The Pantheon
STORY OF
AMERICAN ART
For Young People

PANTHEON BOOKS

The Pantheon STORY OF AMERICAN ART

For Young People

Ariane Ruskin Batterberry and Michael Batterberry

Introduction by Tom Armstrong
DIRECTOR, WHITNEY MUSEUM OF AMERICAN ART

FRONTIS: A City of Fantasy, by an unknown American artist, c. 1850
National Gallery of Art, Washington, D.C.
Gift of Edgar William and Bernice Chrysler Garbisch
CONTENTS: Detail of Snap the Whip, by Winslow Homer, see page 93
INTRODUCTION: Novum Amsterodamum, by Laurens Block, see page 36
PAGE 8: Detail of painted pottery jar, Zia, see page 11

Library of Congress Cataloging in Publication Data
Batterberry, Ariane Ruskin.
The Pantheon story of American art for young people.
SUMMARY: A history of art in the United States which includes the contributions of
the Indians and early settlers and discusses art movements and important individual artists
in the eighteenth, nineteenth, and twentieth centuries.
1. Art, American—History—Juvenile literature. [1. Art, American—History.   2. Artists]
I. Batterberry, Michael, joint author.   II. Title.   N6505.B37   709'.73   75-22249
ISBN 0-394-82842-9   ISBN 0-394-92842-3 lib. bdg.

DESIGNED BY SALLIE BALDWIN

Manufactured in the United States of America

First Edition

ACKNOWLEDGMENTS

We would like to thank the National Gallery of Art, Washington, D.C., the Whitney Museum of American Art,
New York, N.Y., the Collection of Edgar William and Bernice Chrysler Garbisch, the Walker Art Center of
Minneapolis, Minnesota, and the Pace Gallery, New York, N.Y., for their great help in assembling this book. We
would also like to thank J. Carter Brown of the National Gallery of Art, Kathleen Kissane, also of the National
Gallery of Art, Clifford W. Schaefer of the Collection of Edgar William and Bernice Chrysler Garbisch, and Flora
Irving, Margaret Aspinwall, and Anita Duquette of the Whitney Museum, for the personal assistance they have
so generously given in the preparation of *The Pantheon Story of American Art.*

We also want to thank Barbara Novak and Frederick J. Dockstader for their kind and invaluable aid in the
preparation of the text for this book.

Grateful acknowledgment is made for use of the following previously published material:

The color plates on pages 10, 14, 15, 18, 19, 22, 23 from photographs by Eric Sutherland, courtesy Walker Art
Center and The Minneapolis Institute of Arts, from *American Indian Art: Form and Tradition,* 1972.

The color plate on page 27, from a photograph by Alfred A. Blaker, originally published in *Eskimo Masks: Art
and Ceremony* by Dorothy Jean Ray, The University of Washington Press, copyright 1967. Reprinted by permission of The University of Washington Press.

"The Song of the Sky Loom," originally published in *Songs of the Tewa* by Herbert J. Spinden, Exposition of
Indian Tribal Arts, New York, 1933.

"The Great Figure" by William Carlos Williams, *Collected Earlier Poems.* Copyright 1938 by New Directions
Publishing Corporation. Reprinted by permission of New Directions Publishing Corporation.

Excerpts from *Georgia O'Keeffe* by Lloyd Goodrich and Doris Bry, the exhibition catalogue of the Georgia
O'Keeffe retrospective at the Whitney Museum of American Art (1970). Reprinted by permission of the authors and
Whitney Museum of American Art.

CONTENTS

INTRODUCTION

Our country is very young and yet in the relatively brief period of two hundred years since the American Revolution the United States has established an important heritage of cultural accomplishments. Unfortunately, historic developments in American painting and sculpture are generally known only through highlights, and the supreme achievements of American artists in the last twenty-five years are still bewildering to most observers. We have a distant relationship to our art primarily because our education emphasizes classic cultures, the Renaissance, and the development of modernism in Europe.

Too often, as we are taught to appreciate works of art, American artists such as John Singleton Copley, William Sidney Mount, Thomas Eakins, Georgia O'Keeffe, David Smith, Willem de Kooning, and Alexander Calder are not given the prominence accorded artists of other cultures. But our lives are associated with the same background which encouraged their work and a greater knowledge of our history should include an understanding of the creative statements of these and other important American artists.

Artists in the United States during the late eighteenth and nineteenth centuries were confronted with landscapes and frontiers unlike any others in the world. The people who discovered new horizons and settled the country had a determination and vigorous ambition which was translated to us by artists' interpretations of the life and environment of our emerging nation.

The influence of the art of the past upon painters and sculptors during this period in history is one of the most interesting aspects of the story of the growth of the fine arts in America. An understanding of this phase of the development of our cultural heritage is gained through a knowledge of the lives of the artists which are presented with revealing detail in this book.

Painting and sculpture of the twentieth century emerged from the influence of European art and triumphed with the work of abstract expressionists. American art is now the most significant in the world and is understood and respected as much, or more, by connoisseurs in other countries than by those of us privileged to be a part of it. As you begin to understand American art it will give you a new sense of your own individuality. An appreciation of the creative ability of artists will provide you with increased awareness and understanding of your daily experiences.

This splendid book begins with a proper emphasis upon the great art of the American Indian. As you travel through the subsequent history of American art presented so vividly on these pages, the stories about individual artists and the progression of stylistic changes will provide a background for the understanding of their work. It is a great adventure. Eventually the mystery of art will unfold as you become sympathetic to artists' attempts to make original statements and to create unique interpretations through their talents. You will gain insights through their eyes and realize that the artists' great gift to all of us is a special vision and the creative ability to provide the knowledgeable viewer with the opportunity for a continuously renewed sensitivity to life.

TOM ARMSTRONG
Director
Whitney Museum of American Art

New York City
September, 1975

For Adina and Brooks

1
ART OF THE NORTH AMERICAN INDIAN

The Earliest American Artists

When the first European explorers and settlers arrived in America, they found works of art everywhere—paintings, drawings, and designs that they did not understand. This was the art of the American Indian.

We do not know when human beings first came to the continent of North America. We do know that some thirty thousand years ago, the narrow body of water that separates Alaska from Siberia, which we call the Bering Strait, was far shallower than it is today, and small bands of people—hunters in constant search of game—crossed from the plains of Asia to make new homes for themselves in the forests of America. The settlers did not build permanent villages; they roamed far and wide, and ever farther south, until they covered the continents of both North and South America.

These people were artists. They decorated the tools with which they worked and the things

with which they lived. This universal desire of humankind to create objects and to make them as colorful and as beautiful as possible goes back to the earliest times, back to what we call the New Stone Age, perhaps many thousands of years before the first hunters set foot in America. In very early times, the American Indians learned to weave baskets so that they were able to store large amounts of food, and to carry more than they could simply hold in their hands. They found their materials—rushes and reeds, tough long grass, strips of bark, thin twigs that could be bent, vines, and roots—in the forests and plains in which they lived. The pattern of weaving is itself pleasing, but when they could, the Indian weavers dyed the roots and grasses with which they wove so that they could create designs on the surface of their baskets. This done, they attached shells, beads, and even feathers to the baskets for decoration. We can see that the weaver has worked out a

Coiled basket, Klikitat   *The Denver Art Museum*

Painted pottery jar, Zia   *The Museum of the Indian. Heye Foundation*

complicated "geometric" pattern when we look at the coiled basket on the left.

A basket is an excellent container for food, but it will not hold water. Indians in the southwestern part of what later became the United States may have discovered that if they covered their baskets with the soft and clingy earth we call "clay," they became watertight. And wherever people settled down to grow crops on the land, by one means or another, pottery came into being. Moreover, the Indians learned that decorative patterns could easily be scratched, stamped, or pinched in the wet clay, or the potter might attempt a sculpted decoration. They soon found that they could paint decorations on their pottery, using pigments of different-colored earths and a brush made of animal hair. We can only admire the delicate, sharp, and smooth bird design painted on the pot by a woman of the Zia tribe. The

potters discovered, too, that when a clay jar was used for cooking, the heat of the fire made the clay hard and durable. And so they learned to make true ceramics by "firing" their pottery.

From the weaving of baskets it was only a short step to the weaving of other things: mats, traps for fish, and even hammocks. But most important, it was a step toward the weaving of cloth. The Indians of the Southwest, who lived where game was scarce, learned to weave textiles from cotton. Elsewhere, bark, the strings or "fibers" of plants, and even human hair were used. Not all North American Indians wove fabric, however. Where game was plentiful, it was far easier to tan animal skins (particularly deerskin) to form a soft, warm cloth. But everywhere, the American Indians sewed and embroidered, using a needle of finely sharpened bone. Beads were made of clay or polished bone or carefully fashioned from the brightly colored stones we now call "semiprecious." Even a pearl found in the heart of an oyster might be used. And the quills of the porcupine were dyed in bright colors. All these might be sewn in intricate patterns to decorate a dress or suit of clothes, and the feathers of a bird might be sewn onto a splendid headdress.

But when an American Indian created a work of art, he often had very much more in mind than merely making something beautiful. His art had a great deal to do with his religion and his feelings about the world around him. To the Indians, life, and the spirit of life, existed in everything—a tree, a pond, a storm cloud. Even the objects they made with their own hands possessed spirits. When a potter in the Southwest carefully painted a line around a jar, she would leave a break in the line so that the spirit in the jar would be free, and would not be imprisoned by the line. When an Indian warrior was buried, often his weapons and other possessions were buried with him so that they could serve him in the next world. But first these objects, too, would have to be broken, or "killed."

The most powerful, the most important spirits were the all-powerful spirits of nature— the sun, the rain, the wind, the spirits of the animals that were hunted, and many others. Now the Indians felt that they could affect these powerful forces with their words. And so, like the followers of other religions, they offered prayers:

House made of dawn.
House made of evening light.
House made of the dark cloud. . . .
Happily may I walk.
Happily, with abundant dark clouds, may I walk.
Happily, with abundant showers, may I walk.
Happily, with abundant plants, may I walk. . . .
May it be beautiful all around me.
In beauty it is finished.

But the Indians felt, too, that in creating works of art, they could in some way affect the spirits, please them, or work with them, just as they could in creating poetry with words. If an Indian craftsman carved the head of an animal he hunted on a club,

it was to give the club magical power over the animal. And if he painted a ball of the sun on his shirt, he felt it would give him the protection of the sun deity. If an Indian of the Southwest painted a pattern that suggested rain on a jar, she hoped that this would bring rain for her crops.

When a woman of the Plains Indians wished to protect her child from snakebite, she would embroider a zigzag snake pattern on the child's moccasin. Now this pattern does not look like a realistic snake, it only suggests a snake to our minds—it "symbolizes" the snake. There are many such symbols in Indian art. A cross, for example, often symbolizes a star, and a semicircle often represents a mountain. It might, however, represent a cloud to another tribe, just as a zigzag pattern might suggest lightning or gunfire rather than a snake. Every tribe created its own symbols. Originally these drawings may have been realistic, but they were repeated so often that the details were lost and only the pattern of lines remained. Still, this pattern was felt to have the full "magical" force of the realistic picture. Colors, too, might have a symbolic meaning. So the color red might stand for blood (or the earth, or a sunset), blue for the sky, yellow for the sun, or day, and black for night. Not every Indian design had a symbolic meaning, however. Many were devised for their beauty alone.

Of course, not all the works of art that the Indians created were objects for everyday use. The Indians celebrated many religious festivals and ceremonies to honor a birth, a naming, a marriage, a funeral, or for the sake of what was most important in the life of the particular tribe. In the Southwest there were ceremonial prayers for rain, while on the Plains men prayed for the return of the buffalo, and in the Northwest for the return of the salmon. In the East, they prayed for a plentiful crop of corn. Many works of art were created for use in these ceremonies: masks, the painted surfaces of drums, rattles, ornamented costumes, and these were particularly sacred.

Above all, whether the American Indians were creating a poem or a work of art, what was beauty to them was the beauty of nature. All the patterns with which they decorated the objects they loved were taken from nature—a thunderbolt, rocks, a river, a butterfly, a swallow, a lizard. In fact, the Indians saw the beauty of nature in everything. The Anishinabe people measured time by moons—moons of the spirits, moons of the crust of snow, or moons of red berries, the falling leaves, the wild rice. Ten Bears, a chief of the Comanche tribe, welcomed visitors with these words: "My heart is filled with joy, when I see you here, as the brooks fill with water, when the snows melt in the spring, and I feel glad as the ponies do when the fresh grass starts in the beginning of the year."

The Indians of one part of the country led very different lives from those of another. We must remember that they knew no boundary between what later became the United States and Canada, although their world was quite separate from that of the Indians of Mexico.

The People of the Eastern Forests

When the first European settlers arrived from England, Holland, and France, they found the East Coast of North America covered with thick forest. Throughout the woodland lived scattered tribes of Indians. Their villages, fortified by a high wall, consisted of small huts of birch or elm bark, rushes or woven mats, stretched over frames of bent poles. Among the Algonquian people, who lived in the area of the Great Lakes and farther east, these houses were dome shaped. In the area of New York the six nations of the great Iroquois Confederacy (the Oneida, Seneca, Mohawk, Onondaga, Cayuga, and Tuscarora) lived, many families together, in houses that might be a hundred feet long. Their huge, gabled frames were covered with bark. These Indians hunted small game and fished in the many rich rivers of the East. But they were a settled people, and they farmed. It was the Indians of the East Coast who first taught the settlers to grow corn, sweet potatoes, and squash, to eat pumpkins, and to smoke tobacco. They had other lessons to teach as well—how to use seaweed to fertilize the soil, how to bake clams and collect maple sugar and wild rice, and how to build a canoe that could remain afloat on the swiftly rushing streams.

The Indians of the Eastern Woodlands could devote only certain seasons to art. The tribes were constantly at war, and always on the move—from the sugarbushes in the spring to the summer planting ground, with trips to the hunting ground in the winter. It was the women who designed and stitched their fine quillwork embroidery. Porcupine quills were cut into short lengths, dyed in bright natural colors, and embroidered in

Quilled birch bark box, Micmac   *The Museum of the American Indian. Heye Foundation*

False face mask, Iroquois   *The Museum of the American Indian. Heye Foundation*

intricate patterns onto clothing or on objects like the birch bark box from the Micmac tribe (page 13). When quill work was embroidered on leather, the skins were often smoked or dyed a dark brown, or even black, to contrast with the bright colors of the quills.

The men of the eastern Indian tribes were extraordinary carvers of wood. They fashioned not only wooden bowls, spoons, clubs, and other such useful items, but also powerful works of art like the Iroquois masks.

The Onondaga Indians tell the following

tale. One day the Earth Grasper, the creator of humankind and all things, met with a "shaman," a priest who could communicate with the world of the spirits. This shaman was called Hadui, "the great humpbacked one," who had magic powers over game, the winds, and disease. These two vied to show their strength by making a mountain move. The Earth Grasper succeeded and when Hadui spun round to see what had happened, his face struck the newly moved mountain, and his nose and mouth were pushed out of shape. The Earth Grasper recognized Hadui's powers to help

Beaded moccasins, Potawatomi   *Collection of Mrs. O. S. Perkins, Allenspark, Colorado.*
The Denver Art Museum

man, however, and so allowed him to continue to live on earth, although never to be seen. On his part, Hadui promised that if men took on his appearance by wearing a mask of his twisted face, they could use his powers over disease and other ills. So it was that every spring members of the Iroquois Society of Faces, wearing the mask of Hadui, visited each village in turn. The maskers sang, burned tobacco to the spirits, blew the ashes, and recited the legend of Hadui to drive the spirits of disease from anyone who suffered.

The mask of Hadui (page 14) is carved of wood, painted red (these masks were always red or black), and trimmed with horsehair. With its red flesh and pale hair, its staring eyes, and its twisted mouth, it has a strange power. It does not seem extraordinary that the men who wore such masks could perform miracles.

With the coming of the white man, life changed for the forest Indians. Many died of diseases they had not known before, many were killed, and many others fled. As their life changed, so did their art. Above all, the white man brought new materials with which to work. Cloth soon replaced skins for clothing, and metal vessels replaced easily broken pottery. The Indians learned to make brooches, rings, earrings, and bracelets of the white man's silver. But most important, white men brought beads—something which they considered of little worth, but which were valuable to the Indians because they were beautiful. The new beads could be used to create embroidered

Feather headdress (war bonnet), Cheyenne
The Museum of the American Indian. Heye Foundation

designs of brilliant glowing color far more exciting than anything that could be done with porcupine quills, like the floral decoration on a pair of beaded moccasins (page 15). The Indians were eager to trade animal skins for such beads, and the European traders even offered them false *wampum*—made of porcelain in the factories of Europe!

The People of the Plains

When we think of "American Indians," we usually think of a warrior wearing a splendid feather headdress galloping like thunder over the prairies. It may surprise us, then, that no such Indian could be seen in America before the coming of the European settlers.

Why was this? Simply because the European explorers and settlers first brought the horse. Before their arrival, thinly scattered tribes of Indians lived in the forests surrounding the Great Plains that stretched from the Mississippi to the Rockies. These were the Sioux, Crow, Blackfeet, Cheyenne, and many others. They grew corn, beans, squash, and tobacco. At certain times of the year they would make expeditions to the open plain where, with great difficulty, the men would hunt buffalo on foot with bows and stone-headed arrows. All this changed when an expedition of Spanish adventurers, led by Hernando de Soto, set out to explore the Southwest in 1538. Some of de Soto's horses escaped and were captured by the Indians, who soon learned that when they hunted on horseback, the buffalo became easy game. More horses escaped, others were bred, and still others were stolen; and soon the Indians' world changed. Many tribes gave up farming and took to a nomadic life, following the buffalo on horseback and living in tepees, light buffalo-skin tents that could be carried. They lived richly off the buffalo, which they called "big dog." The buffalo's skin was used for making tepees, clothing, bags, jars, and even pots. Tools were made of buffalo bone, and weaving was done with buffalo hair.

The possessions of the Plains Indians were of necessity light and easy to carry. But they had the time and leisure to make of them works of art. The Plains Indians did fine embroidery work with quills and later with beads; they painted tepees, robes, shields, parfleches (bags for storing meat), and containers of every kind—in fact, all their possessions. To own and give rich clothing was a sign of distinction in the tribe.

The tribes' "paint gatherers" collected minerals and other pigments for paints. These were mixed with water or glue, and applied with a brush made of softened bone. The skin to be painted was stretched out on the ground, and the artist crouched over his or her work. Women painted superb "abstract" patterns of lines, circles, and triangles; but the Crow shield (page 18) was painted by a man. Men decorated all the equipment for the hunt, for war, and for religious ceremonies. Men, too, painted realistic figures, like the thunderbird almost hidden by the feathers in the middle of the shield. This figure was supposed to have magical powers, and to be able to attract arrows. The zigzag pattern at the top represented the lightning of bullets. But the Arapaho shirt (page 19) was thought to be bulletproof. It was made to be worn in the Ghost Dance, performed by the Indians of Nevada and Utah at the end of the last century. Here we see a brilliantly starry sky filled with powerful symbols: the waterbird, symbolizing water, which was so precious to these Indians, and the turtle, who was invincible because of his strong armor. The purpose of the Ghost Dance was to drive away the white people, to make them magically disappear. The small human figures at the neck represent the white people's god, who must also come to the aid of the Indian.

The People of the Southwest

When the first European settlers arrived on the East Coast of North America, they had little idea that an extraordinary group of Indians lived in the far Southwest—Indians who lived in towns made up of hundreds of stone houses, and who wove textiles as fine as any in Europe. These were the Pueblo tribes first seen by the Spanish explorer Francisco Vásquez de Coronado.

Painted shield, Crow   *The Museum of the American Indian. Heye Foundation*

Ghost dance shirt, Arapaho   *The Museum of the American Indian. Heye Foundation*

A thousand years before the Spanish came, these tribes, the Hopi, Zuñi, and others, lived in dwellings called "pueblos," made of many one-room houses massed together into one huge building, arranged in terraces. The walls of these stone buildings were plastered with adobe (dried mud), and they looked very like a pile of children's blocks, or a piece of sculpture, with smooth surfaces catching the light at different angles. The largest of these huge "apartment" houses, Pueblo Benito, had no less than four hundred rooms on four floors. Pueblos were built for defense against wandering tribes, and so there were no doors on the ground floor—they were entered by ladders that could be pulled up quickly.

The pueblo dwellers and other Indians of the Southwest were not hunters. They tilled the fields near their settlements, and where there was not enough water, they dug ditches for irrigation. The materials with which they lived and worked were different from those of the Indians farther east. They had fewer animal pelts and less wood; but they had splendid clay, with which they made superb pottery like the jar we have seen, decorated in clean, smooth geometrical lines, often in shades of red, black, and white. Nor did they need skins for clothing. From earliest times they wove cloth on a kind of loom. Native cotton was grown, and the weavers created patterns with strands of contrasting colors. Sometimes these fabrics were as delicate as lace. When the Spanish came, the Indians learned to breed sheep and use their wool for weaving. The blanket on the opposite page belonged to the great Apache chief Geronimo, who raided the New Mexico and Arizona territories at the end of the last century. Geronimo, in turn, gave the blanket to "Doc" Demarest, a railroad surveyor and veternarian, who had cured the Chief's favorite horse. The blanket was a handsome gift—brilliantly patterned in green, yellow, and black on red. The Navaho created such blankets by unraveling European wool cloth and reweaving the thread in the patterns they preferred.

Pueblo in Taos, New Mexico   *Bureau of Indian Affairs, Department of the Interior*

Blanket belonging to Apache chief Geronimo   *Collection, Mr. Robert Rubin*

Dance mask, Pueblo   *Collected by Amelia E. White. Cranbrook Institute of Science*

The most fascinating art of the Indians of the Southwest played a part in their religious beliefs. To them, religion was of the greatest importance. The men of the Hopi tribe actually devoted more than half their time to religious ceremonies and dances. Of most importance was the Kachina cult. The Kachinas were thought to be spirits, divine beings with powers over rain, crops, clouds, the wind, and many other forces. The Kachinas lived high in the mountains in summer, but in the winter they lived among the people. They were the go-betweens who told the gods of the people's wishes and problems. In religious ceremonies, men wearing Kachina masks like the one seen here became the spirits themselves. It is in fact a helmet made of painted leather and wood, with slits for eyes. Others might have a collar of fur or spruce leaves. We can tell that it is very different from the Iroquois mask we have seen. The face of the Iroquois mask was far from "realistic." Here there is no true face at all, only a geometrical design. Yet such "abstract"

Cloud kachina doll, Hopi   *The Denver Art Museum*

designs, as we call them, represented things that were very real to the Indians. Here the stepped pattern on the cheeks of the mask symbolizes the all-encircling mountains. On either side of the head, lightning falls from semicircular clouds, while the larger semicircles represent mountains as high as the clouds.

Look also at the Kachina doll above. These little figures were made every year for the children of the tribe. They represented the Kachinas they

Carved and painted wood canoe ornament, Tlingit *Field Museum of Natural History, Chicago*

had seen in the yearly ceremonies, masks and all, and were meant to teach children about their religion. This Kachina represents the spirit of the clouds. On the face we see only two lines for eyes and one for a mouth. The stepped forms that spring out and above the headdress represent mountains, and the semicircles are clouds. On the cheeks we see clouds that rain like tears. At first this may seem strange to us, but if we study the figure, we will see that it does, indeed, remind us of high peaks and great puffs of piled-up clouds, just such mountains and clouds as one might see clearly in the blue sky over the desert.

The people of the Southwest lived especially close to their gods. And they felt that their art was close to the art of the gods. Hear, for example, "The Song of the Sky Loom." To the Tewa Indians, the soft, light desert raindrops were like threads falling from a loom in the sky:

> O our Mother the Earth, O our Father the Sky
> Your children are we, and with tired backs
> We bring you the gifts you love.
> Then weave for us a garment of brightness;
> May the warp be the white light of morning,
> May the weft be the red light of evening,
> May the fringes be the falling rain,
> May the border be the standing rainbow.
> Thus weave for us a garment of brightness,
> That we may walk fittingly where birds sing,
> That we may walk fittingly where grass is green,
> O our Mother the Earth, O our Father the Sky.

The Indians of the Northwest Coast

The last Indians discovered by the European settlers as they pushed west from New England and north from California were the Indians of the Northwest Coast (running from Oregon to Alaska). And in many ways they were the most extraordinary. The Indians of the Northwest Coast were separated from the rest of the continent by the high ranges of the Rockies. They lived where thick forests led to a rocky shore with many rivers and inlets. Fish was plentiful—they did not bother to grow food—and wood provided them with every other need. They used wood cleverly, as the Plains Indians used the buffalo. Red cedar was their favorite, and they used its bark to weave mats, clothing, and even a kind of waterproof poncho. Their houses were built of wood, as were their high, seagoing dugout canoes, which might hold forty to fifty people. Above all, they were great carvers of wood, who decorated everything they possessed. An example is the carved and painted ornament (page 23) for one

of their great canoes, a winged spirit to challenge any danger.

With plenty of food, the Indians of the Northwest Coast led a leisurely life. They had time to think of other things—not only art, but also social position in the tribe.

The tribe was divided into three groups—chiefs, freemen, and slaves—and a member's place in society was thought to be of great importance. One's position depended partly on one's wealth in beautifully decorated possessions, and partly on one's ancestry, according to the myths and legends of the tribe.

A member of the tribe best established importance and social position by giving a *potlach* (which is an Indian word meaning "gift"). This was a ceremonial feast for some occasion such as a marriage or the birth of a son. The host would show his great wealth by distributing gifts to his guests. He might give away hundreds of blankets, like the one we see here. It is woven into complicated patterns with threads of cedar bark and the wool of the mountain goat, and it is meant to represent the ferocious spirit of a killer whale. Or the host might present a guest with a copper shield (the Indians of the Northwest knew how to work copper) worth perhaps ten thousand such blankets. The guests were expected to return gifts of as great, or even greater value. Moreover, in a show of sheer wealth, the host might choose simply to burn his possessions in public. In that case, the guests were expected to burn their possessions in return.

The Indians of the Northwest Coast often lived in large wooden houses with pitched roofs. As many as fifty members of the same clan or family group might live together. In front of the house there often stood a totem pole. Now, among these Indians (and many other American Indians), it was believed that a person or family might bear a kinship to, or be a close relative of, a certain animal or mythical being. So it was told that the ancestor of the Bear clan was a woman who was captured by the king of the bears. Before she was rescued by hunters, she bore a child who was half human and half bear. The ancestor of the Eagle clan was an eagle who came to earth

Woven mountain-goat hair blanket, Chilkat   *The Museum of the American Indian. Heye Foundation*

and turned himself into a human being, except for his beak. Such an animal then, was sacred to the clan—its *totem*. It would appear in the clan's songs, dances, and masks, and on its totem pole.

The totem pole was the insignia of the clan. For those who could read its meaning, it told the story of the clan or its chief. The intertwined carvings of beasts and men on a totem pole tell the myths, legends, and historical events in the family's history. The totem pole here was carved of cedarwood for Chief Eagle of Kasaan Village, a member of the Haida tribe that lives in Alaska. It is huge—more than forty-three feet tall—and it tells of the chief's family heritage and hunting exploits. At the top we see the eagle, the chief's totem. Beneath are prestige cylinders, indicating the chief's importance and adding height to the pole. Beneath we see the figure of a grizzly bear, another ancestor of the chief, who was also descended from the Bear clan, and beneath this we see the king of the bears attacking his human

Totem pole, Haida   *The Museum of the American Indian. Heye Foundation*

Wooden mask of an old woman, Niska   *The Museum of the American Indian. Heye Foundation*

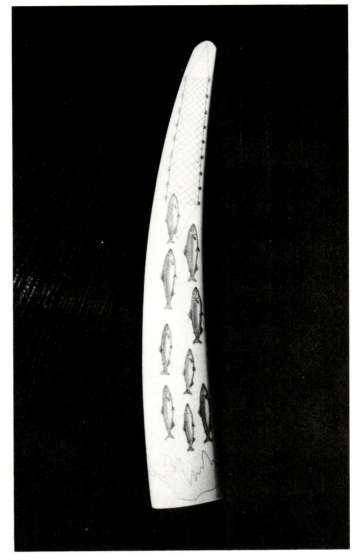

Engraved walrus tusk, Eskimo   *The Museum of the American Indian. Heye Foundation*

wife, the chief's ancestor. Beneath these stand a frog person and a beaver, telling us that the chief or a close relative had married a member of the Beaver clan. And at the very bottom, in the grasp of the powerful animal spirits, we see the tiny figure of the hunter.

Let us look closely at this totem pole. It was carved well after the first European traders had brought metal knives to the Northwest, when Indian carving, always very fine, became finer still. The figures, with heads much larger than their bodies, are far from realistic. In fact, it is difficult to tell which are human, and which are animal. The features of both have been broken down into a pattern of brightly painted planes. The same is true of the faces and symbolic figures we have already seen in the killer whale blanket. These are spirits, more strong and powerful

than life, and different from it. When, generation after generation, artists represent certain things in a set and unchanging way which is not realistic, but which represents reality to them, we say their art is *stylized,* and this was true of the art of the Indians of the Northwest Coast. But we must not think they could not represent things realistically. Look at the mask of the old woman above. The anatomy of the face is perfect— it is carefully modeled and very real. With its deep wrinkles, missing teeth, and straggly hair, it is a vivid portrait of old age itself.

The Eskimos

We have said that the Indians of the Northwest lived along the Pacific Coast from Oregon to Alaska, including present-day Canada. Still farther north, in Alaska and the arctic part of Canada and Greenland, live the Eskimo. These people roam at the very edges of the ice cap, hunting the walrus and whale with weapons of bone. For centuries their life was a lonely one—they saw the green earth for only a few months a year, and in winter they lived in huts of driftwood and sand, or in igloos built from the ice itself. In those long months when the sun scarcely shone, their only warmth and light came from a lamp of whale fat, lit by a wick of moss. And yet the Eskimos were artists. During the long winter nights they carved pieces of whalebone and walrus tusk into finely worked shapes. They liked to engrave or paint scenes of their life, showing figures of other men and animals that they saw so rarely and that meant so much to them, like the salmon fishing scene carved on the tusk at left. For their religious ceremonies, they created masks as strange, fantastic, and delightful as any made by the people farther south.

The bold mask below was worn by a shaman. It represents the sun, the moon, and helping dog spirits. The sun throws wide its hands in a generous gesture. On either side of the sun's brilliant

Carved and painted wood shaman's mask, Eskimo *Lowie Museum of Anthropology,*
University of California, Berkeley

face hover the circles of the moon. Above are the heads of the helping dog spirits, and their floppy ears are at the four corners of the mask. We must remember that, to the Eskimo, his friend the dog was very important. Dogs pulled the Eskimos' sled great distances over the ice in search of game, helped in the hunt, and warmed their masters. And when we look at this mask we can almost feel the chill of nature that the Eskimo was made to face. Like other natives of the Americas, the Eskimos put their feelings into their poetry:

O warmth of summer sweeping over the land.
Not a breath of wind,
Not a cloud,
And among the mountains
The grazing caribou,
The dear caribou,
In the blue distance.
O how entrancing,
O how joyful,
I lay me on the ground, sobbing . . .

The Mound Builders

Few of the objects made by the American Indians that we have seen are very old. The climate of much of North America is damp; baskets of straw, wooden carvings, and clothing made of animal skins decay quickly. Have the Indians always lived the same way, since first they came to North America? The truth is that we know very little about the past of the Indians, and they themselves did not keep written records. But in the Southeast, there is an inkling of history. At some point, perhaps two thousand years ago, an extraordinary people whom we call simply the Mound Builders lived in the Ohio and Mississippi valleys.

The Mound Builders (this is the only name we have for them) followed a simple farming life and lived in thatched cottages with walls of mud. But what amazes us is that they built enormous mounds constructed of rubble and topped with earth. The largest of these, called Monk's Mound, near East Saint Louis, Illinois, is no less than

Serpent Mound, near Locust Grove, Ohio   *Courtesy of the Ohio Historical Society*

Carved bowl representing male wood duck, from Hale County, Alabama, circa 1300–1600 *The Museum of the American Indian. Heye Foundation*

1000 feet long, 700 feet wide, and a full 100 feet tall. Many such mounds were used as the burial places of chiefs but others, like this one, probably served as a kind of base or platform for some sacred building such as a temple or the palace of a ruler. Most astonishing are the "effigy mounds," man-made hills of enormous size built in the shape of animals. The true effect of these can only be appreciated from the air. A remarkable one is the Serpent Mound built in Ohio. From the air we see that it has the form of a gracefully curling snake. Yet it would be difficult to make out this form from the ground—it is a full fifth of a mile in length. These Mound Builders were also craftsmen who could carve figures from the hardest stone, like the bowl in the form of a wood duck, using only instruments of stone or bone, or the friction of sand. From it we can tell how closely they studied nature and how much they enjoyed it.

Who were the Mound Builders? Were they ancestors of the Indians that the first settlers found in the Middle West? Or were they a people who died and left no trace? We do not know. It may be that the last of the Mound Builders were still at work when the very first explorers arrived, or it may be that they were the ancestors of today's Creek-Caddo people. But by the time European settlers came to build their homesteads in the Ohio and Mississippi valleys, the Mound Builders had long since gone and their very existence was unknown. To these early settlers, the Indians of the Eastern Woodlands and the Plains, with their masks and shields, their pottery and embroidery, were mystery enough.

The Indians had created a world of color and decorative beauty out of the American wilderness. But it was so totally strange to the European settlers that they did not recognize its beauty, or seek to learn its meaning. They saw both the Indians and the wilderness as something that must be conquered. For almost three centuries—centuries during which the Indian artists created some of their finest works—white men would be blind to Indian art. The earliest settlers, meanwhile, had brought with them their own art, from the cozy little villages and bustling towns and cities of England, Holland, France, and Spain, thousands of miles away.

2
ART OF THE FIRST SETTLERS

The English Settlers

What was the "New World" that greeted the first settlers really like? To begin with, it was covered with a thick forest of pine, maple, and oak, so thick that the settlers could smell it while still out at sea, long before they sighted land. There were no roads through this forest, only the narrow footpaths of the Indians; and before crops could be planted, fields would have to be cleared with back-breaking effort. Yet the forest teamed with game. It must have seemed a paradise to settlers from England where few forests remained, and where a poacher could be put to death for killing a deer on a nobleman's property. The land blossomed with new flowers, fruits, and berries. The soil, when it was cleared, proved to be rich. Still there were many things to terrify the settler: swamps and jungles to the south, mosquitoes that stung, and wild animals—wolves, panthers, and bears—that had long since disappeared from most of Europe. And above all there were the Indians,

people whose curious ways seemed beyond understanding and who might be friendly and helpful, or who might attack.

And so it is no surprise that the first English settlers tried to re-create, as closely as they could, the lives they had lived at home. They built little villages with tiny gardens and gabled houses, often cramped close together in the English style, although they had an entire continent in which to spread. Before the century was out, large and handsome homes such as the John Ward House were to be found in new and thriving communities like Salem. In the North these homes were built of wood with clapboard sides and brick chimneys, but in the South whole houses were built of brick. Within, one low room often served many purposes. Let us look inside a room from the Thomas Hart house in Ipswich, Massachusetts.

The sturdy oak beams that support the ceiling can be seen clearly. The walls are constructed

John Ward house, Salem, Massachusetts   *Courtesy of Essex Institute, Salem, Massachusetts*

of sun-dried brick. One wall is covered by a paneling of wooden boards, but the others are faced with plaster, which was often made of clay mixed with hair. A large fireplace is hung with pots for cooking, but it also warms the house. Over the fire there often hung a bed warmer, too, which was certainly a comfort in cold New England winters. The room must have been smoky much of the time. It was Benjamin Franklin who first invented a fireplace that really drew successfully. The few pieces of furniture are very well made: a simple bedstead, a cradle, a table, a few stools,

Parlor from the Thomas Hart house, built about 1640, Ipswich, Massachusetts
The Metropolitan Museum of Art

The "Carver" armchair, mid 17th century
Philadelphia Museum of Art: The Charles F. Williams Collection

and a handsome cupboard in which all the family's possessions were stored. There is only one chair, to be used by older members of the family and a few honored guests. Because space was small, the seat of a chair might be a storage box, and its back might lower to become a table. Some of the furniture might be elaborately carved, like the maple armchair you see here. This is in a style called "Jacobean" because it was popular in England during the reigns of James I and James II. The room may seem somber, but often such Puritan rooms were full of color. The walls or pieces of furniture might be brightly painted, and there were lively colored cushions to soften the chairs and benches. In this room the table is covered with a colorful "turkey work" rug (a Turkish carpet), and the curtains on the windows

(made of small diamond-shaped panes of glass) are cranberry red homespun wool. Stepping outside, the settler would see the streets of his town decorated with brightly painted signs.

We must remember that everything the settlers possessed they were forced to make themselves. Only a few precious things, such as some fine china, a clock, or an illustrated book, could be brought by ship from Europe. But the Puritans came from homes in the English countryside where families were used to doing their own spinning, sewing, and carpentering. Many were craftsmen, and they brought their crafts with them. There were turners, joiners, carpenters, smiths, millers, coopers (makers of barrels), and shoemakers. The first settlers in New England brought their artists and their art, as everything else, with them. These first artists were also craftsmen. They were called "limners" (meaning "liners"), and a "limner" did not paint only pictures, he painted many things—furniture, coaches, and even signs.

One might think that in the great struggle with the wilderness an artist was not important, but this was far from true. The artists, more than any other craftsmen, brought what was graceful, charming, and beautiful in the Old World to the New. Not many of the pictures they painted for the colonists have been found, but those that do remain tell us a great deal about the settlers' life and the way they thought and felt.

The few paintings that remain from the early English colonies are all portraits. Why should that be? We must remember that paintings of the new wilderness and its people did not interest the settlers—they had quite enough of it around them. Within their homes, they wanted everything to remind them of England. But we must remember, too, that the settlers of the Massachusetts Bay Colony were all Puritans; it was their burning belief in their own faith that led them to come to the New World. They did not believe in the "wordly" decoration of the Anglican churches (as those of the Church of England were called), and they did not approve of painting "images" to be worshiped. The Puritans held their religious services in simple, unadorned meeting-houses, so there could be no painting of religious subjects. But as the colony prospered, with milling, weaving, shipbuilding, and trade in lumber and fish, the wealthy merchants of Massachusetts Bay wanted greater comfort and decoration in their homes. One form of painting of which they did approve was the painting of portraits. In America, where people were few and the wilderness without end, every man, woman, and child counted, and their likenesses were worth keeping.

Let us look at the portrait of *Mrs. Freake and Baby Mary* (page 34), painted about 1674. It is hard to believe that such soft and gentle creatures could survive in the harsh wilderness of America, yet they did. They not only survived, they prospered. The artist has carefully painted every detail of Mrs. Freake's starched linen and her delicate lace collar. We often think of the Puritans as somber people, but Mrs. Freake is not this way at all. Her dress is trimmed with bright ribbons and her underskirt is of a rich red brocade. Baby Mary, who stretches her arms to her mother, looks like a small adult, and is dressed as one.

To us these paintings may seem flat. There are no shadows to give the sitters a rounded appearance. And the figures themselves seem stiff. Moreover, their anatomy does not seem quite correct. The hand, are not properly drawn, and Baby Mary could not actually be resting on her mother's knee as she appears. This style of painting was English, but it was not the style of the English court. Many, if not all, of the artists painting in America in 1674 had been taught in England, and some had little training. Also, they had learned their trade in the western counties from which the Puritans came. There, artists still painted as they had almost a century earlier, when Elizabeth I was still queen. This was the style that Elizabeth had preferred. She did not like shadows. To her they looked like smudges on the face.

American families loved to have their children painted. Look at the portrait of *Alice Mason* (page 35). As in the other paintings we have seen, she is portrayed against a simple dark background. The "perspective" lines of the checkered floor at her feet give the picture a feeling of depth. She is obviously behaving herself for the painter, and stands rather stiffly. Like Baby Mary, she is dressed as an adult. This was the fashion in the seventeenth century, a time when many children were expected to behave as adults, caring for younger children or helping their parents by doing whatever work they could. And yet Alice Mason is gentle and appealing. She seems real despite the stiff heavy clothing that encloses her and the sense of importance the artist has made her feel.

If American artists could portray children, they could portray the elderly as well. *Anne Pollard* (page 35) was one hundred years old when she posed for her portrait in 1721. According to her own story, at the age of ten, when "a romping girl," she was the first person to jump boldly off the ship when Governor Winthrop's party of settlers founded Salem. The land, which later became Boston, was "very uneven, abounding in small hollows and swamps, covered with blueberries and other bushes." She lived to see it grow into a city, where she kept a tavern and gave birth to twelve children. When the portrait was painted, she had no less than a hundred and thirty descendants. We can see a century of hardship and struggle in her face. Still, with her thin lips, sagging cheeks, and wise old eyes, we sense she is a crusty soul, well able to help found a nation.

Who were the artists who were able to create portraits so real that the early settlers come alive for us, and so charming and colorful that they brought warmth and beauty to their hard and often bitter lives? Few of the paintings are signed, and what records we have do not tell us. Today the painter of the Freake family is called simply the "Freake limner," and the artist who painted the Mason children is called the "Mason limner." It may be that all these pictures were painted by the same person. Certainly, an artist like this one might well travel from town to town, wherever his talents were needed.

The Dutch Settlers

We have been speaking of the earliest English settlers in North America, but it was the Dutch who came to New Amsterdam to trade and to

Mrs. Freake and Baby Mary, by an unknown artist, c. 1674   *Worcester Art Museum, Worcester, Massachusetts.*
Gift of Mr. and Mrs. Albert W. Rice

Alice Mason, by an unknown artist, 1670
*U.S. Department of the Interior, National
Park Service, Adams National Historical Site*

Anne Pollard, by an unknown artist,
1721   *Courtesy Massachusetts
Historical Society*

Novum Amsterodamum, by Laurens Block, 1650   *Courtesy of the New-York Historical Society, New York City*

manage huge tracts of land granted to them by their government. Like the English, the Dutch brought their homeland with them. New Amsterdam soon appeared like any Dutch town, with small canals and winding streets and brick houses topped by the curious stepped gables that are seen often in Holland. The new town was very colorful. Many houses were decorated with glazed bricks in shades of pink, yellow, orange, purple, or blue. And it was scrubbed clean. An amazed Puritan visitor from New England wrote: "They keep their houses cleaner than their bodies, and their bodies cleaner than their souls." He remarked that the Dutch not only washed their floors daily, they actually scoured them with sand.

The Dutch adored art, and their attitudes were not at all those of the Puritans. At home they covered their walls with paintings of every sort—portraits, still lifes, landscapes, seascapes, and scenes of battles on land and sea. They also liked what are called "genre" paintings, pictures of everyday life—a cobbler at his bench, a family party, or a man enjoying a tankard of beer. These were painted in a style that was extremely realistic in every detail, and the Dutch painters more than any others in the seventeenth century tried to capture a sense of space and true light. Dutch paintings were usually small easel pictures that were easy to transport. One settler, Dr. de Lang, a barber-surgeon, actually brought his entire collection of sixty-one paintings with him to the New World.

The Dutch did not seem to be very inter-ested in painting the wilderness. Like their English neighbors, they wanted to escape it. But as soon as New Amsterdam looked like a corner of Holland, they painted it. The picture above is a watercolor, painted in 1650, showing New Amsterdam as a sleepy port with ships idling gracefully in its harbor. The artist was one Laurens Block, and his picture, like a true Dutch landscape, is a scene of misty and graceful charm. The Dutch, too, appreciated portraits. Looking at the stern face of New Amsterdam's governor, Peter Stuyvesant, you can tell what steely stuff the old governor, who ruled like a despot, was made of.

Peter Stuyvesant, attributed to Henri Couturier, active 1660–84   *Courtesy of the New-York Historical Society, New York City*

Virgin Annunciate (New Mexico Retalbo), 19th century *National Gallery of Art, Washington, D.C. Index of American Design. Watercolor rendering by E. Boyd*

The Spanish Settlers

The Dutch and English colonists, as they struggled to clear the forest of the Eastern Seaboard, had little thought for the Spanish settlers on the other side of the continent—a continent that was far more difficult to cross than the ocean. We must remember that the Spanish had built great cities with palaces and cathedrals long before the Pilgrims set out for New England in the *Mayflower*. The Spanish pushed north into the present-day United States as well, and would have ruled Florida had they not been driven out by the French in the sixteenth century. But they did settle in present-day California, Arizona, and New Mexico, and the city of Santa Fe was founded in 1609. The Spanish came not so much to farm as to hunt for treasure and convert the Indians to Catholicism. The most important buildings in any settlement were the palace of the governor and the church. Let us look at the church of San Esteban Rey at Acoma Pueblo in New Mexico. We can see immediately that it looks like a pueblo itself. The Spanish were not nearly as interested in re-building Europe on American soil as were the settlers in the East. The church is like most Spanish churches, with bell towers on either side of the main building. But it was constructed by Indians of adobe bricks, just as the pueblos were, and like them it looks as if it were part of the desert.

The painting of the *Virgin Annunciate* is from the altar of such a church. At first glance it may seem flat or crudely painted, and clearly the artist was self-taught. But the Madonna's peace as she cherishes the dove can give us some idea of the simple faith of the Southwest.

Church of San Esteban Rey at Acoma Indian Pueblo, New Mexico, c. 1642 *Photo Courtesy of New Mexico State Department of Development*

3
THE EIGHTEENTH CENTURY

The Colonial Home

During the eighteenth century the American colonies grew at a tremendous rate. By the year 1700, a quarter of a million people had made new homes for themselves in the New World. At the time of the Revolution, almost two and a half million people lived in the colonies, which were no longer a wilderness. Great cities had grown up. Philadelphia, with a population of forty thousand, was the second largest city in the British Empire. Boston and New York were not far behind.

As the colonies grew and spread, they became wealthier. On the small farms in the North, orchards burst with fruit, vegetable patches grew, and livestock fattened on the hay and corn. In the South, there were great plantations of tobacco, rice, and indigo (a plant producing a valuable blue dye). The cities' craftsmen—carpenters, candlers, coopers, shoemakers, weavers, tailors, and such—were busy at work, while merchants made fortunes trading with the East Indies and with

England. It was a land where a man who started life as an indentured servant might hope to win a vast fortune—far larger than his master's. But there was enough for everyone. In the eighteenth century Americans were better housed and surely better fed than any people in the world.

The newly wealthy settlers, naturally enough, wanted elegant houses in which to live and public buildings of which they could be proud. For this they followed the "Georgian" fashion set in England (that is, the architectural style of the reign of the four King Georges, covering most of the eighteenth century). In America, buildings were constructed in a "Colonial" style that was simpler, but very much the same. If we look at the painting of George Washington's home, Mount Vernon, we can see that it is a very different place from the John Ward house. A lower, "hipped" roof has replaced the tall gables. Instead of small, unevenly placed windows, all is "sym-

A View of Mount Vernon, the
Seat of General Washington, by
an unknown artist, c. 1790 or later
*National Gallery of Art, Washington, D.C. Gift of Edgar William
and Bernice Chrysler Garbisch*

metrical," which is to say that one side balances the other exactly. The doors are centered, and the windows are of the same size on each floor, and equally far apart. Colonial architects, like the Georgian architects in England, tended to decorate their buildings with details taken from the architecture of Greece and Rome, such as the triangular "pediment" supported by columns that often fronted the porch of Greek or Roman temples. If we look closely at the picture of Mount Vernon, we can see columns at either side of the front door, supporting a triangular pediment over

the door itself. The triangle of the pediment is repeated in the roof. Although most English Georgian houses were built of stone, many Colonial houses, no matter how large, were constructed of wood, as was Mount Vernon.

Looking inside a handsome Colonial house, we can see at a glance how much American life changed in the hundred years since the first settlers had built their homes. The room from Almodington, a house in Somerset County, Maryland, is handsome and airy, and the ceiling high. The fireplace is still important, but now it is sur-

Room from Almodington, Maryland, c. 1750   *The Metropolitan Museum of Art*

rounded by a handsome mantle, with tall pilasters (flattened Roman columns) standing on either side. Elegant paneling covers the plaster and beams, and a framed picture hangs on the wall. On either side of the fireplace, cupboards with glass doors are set into the wall. The paneling is a soft gray-green, very popular in the eighteenth century; the walls inside the cupboard are painted raspberry, and the shelves trimmed with gold. Luxury glistens everywhere. Fine furniture, in the delicate style popular in eighteenth-century England, shines with a high polish. Many pieces are made of a rare wood, mahogany, brought from the Indies and prized for its rich, dark color. Glassware and silver glitter, and fine china shines brightly from where it has been set on display within the cupboard.

The fine china came by ship—from the great factories of Worcester, in England, or from China itself. But the furniture and silver are of American make. Of course, American cabinetmakers followed general English designs. And the eighteenth century was a period when the English were par-

Silver Tankard, made by Paul Revere, Boston, 1795 *The Metropolitan Museum of Art. Bequest of A. T. Clearwater, 1933*

Highboy, Philadelphia, c. 1765 *The Metropolitan Museum of Art. Kennedy Fund, 1918*

ticularly well known for their furniture designers —Chippendale, Sheraton, Hepplewhite, and the Adam brothers. But American workmanship was so fine that it often cannot be told from the best that the English had to offer. The high chest (or highboy) is an excellent example of American cabinetmaking. Such a tall chest (really two chests, one on top of the other), balanced on gracefully turned legs, was an American invention, made only in the colonies. We can admire, too, the beautiful proportions and the fine strong curve of a silver tankard made in America. Its maker was Paul Revere, Jr., the best silversmith in Boston and son of a master silversmith of French descent, Paul Revere, Sr., whose name was originally Rivoire.

Eighteenth Century Portraits

In art, as in everything else, English fashions were followed throughout the colonies, even though many of the new settlers were not English. As we remember, the earliest American painters came from the back country of England and knew nothing of court art. But now that American merchants had become rich, and traveled often to London, they wanted this very court style in the portraits of themselves and their families. They needed pictures that would look suitable in their splendid paneled drawing rooms.

What was this court style? It was the style of the painter Van Dyke and his imitators, Sir Peter Lely and Sir Godfrey Kneller. This style was very different from anything yet seen in the colonies. All is drama, graceful movement—so different from the quiet of the Mason children. The figures are in deep shadow and the rich taffetas, velvets, and laces they wear seem to flow with motion. Behind them the artist painted, not a flat darkness, but light and a background that suggests wealth and importance. These pictures were in fact the product of an entire factory of artists. The master often painted no more than the face. The rest would be filled in by assistants —one painted only hands, another laces, another wigs, and several did the background. Such paintings rarely reached America. But there were many engravings of court portraits, and these were circulated and carefully studied by artists in the colonies who used them as models for the portraits they painted.

The first artist in America who tried his hand at the court style was one Thomas Smith, a sea captain who arrived from Bermuda in 1650, and who painted toward the end of the seventeenth century. He could not have had much formal training, as we can tell from this portrait of his daughter, *Maria Catherine Smith*. Here are the deep shadows and moving drapery. She is a worldly young woman in a low-cut dress, quite like a lady of the court, and not at all like Mrs. Freake. But the painting seems crudely done. The draperies do not fall in a way that makes sense; the light does not melt gently into the shadows, but contrasts with them sharply. Other American

Maria Catherine Smith, by Thomas Smith, c. 1690–1700   *Courtesy, American Antiquarian Society*

Mary Bonticou Lathrop, by John Durand, c. 1770   *The Metropolitan Museum of Art.*
Gift of Edgar William and Bernice Chrysler Garbisch, 1962

artists, who received a bit more training, were better able to solve some of these problems.

Sometimes American artists imitated a few favorite English engravings so closely that many of their paintings look exactly alike. For example, the portrait of *Mr. Van Vechten* and the portrait of *Mr. Willson* (page 44) could almost be the same painting. Two men, wearing identical clothing, stand in almost the same pose. Strangely, we do not even know whether these pictures are by the same artist. But we do know that they were modeled on the same English engraving. The details differ, however, and these we should read like a book. Both men are elegantly dressed, with

Lady with Beaded Headdress, attributed to J. Cooper, c. 1718   *Philadelphia Museum of Art.*
Gift of Edgar William and Bernice Chrysler Garbisch

well-tailored coats and fine linen at the neck and wrists. This tells us that they are wealthy, and not to be confused with back-country farmers in their homespun cloth, or craftsmen in their leather aprons. Each man stands by an open window, a sort of "symbolic" window into his life. Through Mr. Van Vechten's we see a neat row of trees, which suggests that he is a landowner. Mr. Willson's looks out onto the sea and a ship at full sail. Mr. Willson must surely be a merchant or a sea captain. That he carries a hat and sword would tell us that he is a military or naval man. Mr. Van Vechten has neither. He must be a farmer, as he holds forward two stalks of wheat. Are these paintings simply imitations of English works, telling us each man's profession, like a sign or label? No, they are more. If we look at the faces we realize they are not copied from anything the artist had seen but from life itself. They are straightforward portraits of men of the New

Mr. Willson, by an unknown artist, 1720 *National Gallery of Art, Washington, D.C. Gift of Edgar William and Bernice Chrysler Garbisch.*

Mr. Van Vechten, by an unknown artist, 1719 *National Gallery of Art, Washington, D.C. Andrew Mellon Collection*

World. These are not lackadaisical, spoiled, or bored aristocrats, but strong men, with faces that are far from perfect and with fire in their eyes. John Durand's portrait of *Mary Bonticou Lathrop* (page 42) gives us the same feeling. The expensive silks and laces are there, but little attention has been paid to them. What is more important is the clear-eyed, forthright expression on the girl's face.

The artists who painted these portraits had a certain amount of training and studied foreign engravings with care. Such artists traveled from one city to another. Deep in the country, far from the towns, other artists were at work.

Lady with Beaded Headdress (page 43) was found in Katonah, New York. It may have been the work of a little known artist of English background, one J. Cooper, and it dates from perhaps 1718. Clearly, no such lady as this, in the jeweled tiara, the ermines, and the silks of the English court, was to be seen deep in the Hudson Valley. But Cooper must have seen a print of a portrait of such a lady, a print made from an English painting. With no more knowledge of how the original was painted than Thomas Smith possessed a generation earlier, he tried, with broad strokes of flat color, to reproduce it. We can tell that he has scarcely succeeded, but the picture pleased the settlers of the valley, and the great lady must have appealed to their imagination. In the painting of *Catherine Hendrickson* by a New Jersey artist, we again have the feeling that we are looking at a fairy-tale princess in a never-never world of strange flowers and beasts. And so it was with so many eighteenth-century American portraits. We see men and women, regally dressed, at play in a dreamland of formal gardens, or commanding splendid views of ships at sea. What we do not see is America as it actually was, not an endless formal garden but a vast wilderness where Indians were still a threat. Nor do we see the back-breaking toil of the settlers, most of whom wove their own cloth, and all of whom milked their own cows, baked their own bread, churned their own butter, used birchbark for paper, and went to bed at nightfall to save on the expense of candles. No matter how wealthy, the settlers were never far from this world, except in their dreams and in the paintings. Even here, we see reality in their faces—in their eyes.

Once in a while, however, the world as the settlers honestly saw it crept into their art. We can see this below in a portrait of an Indian by Gustavus Hesselius, a Swedish artist who came to Virginia with his brother, a minister. Hesselius wanted to avoid the "airs and graces" so popular in his time. The Indian he has painted was a man of importance, a chief of the Lenni-Lenape tribe called Lapowinsa (Going Away to Gather Food). At the moment the portrait was painted, John Penn, the Proprietor of Pennsylvania, was trying to persuade him to sell a large piece of Indian territory. In fact, Penn intended to cheat him. The Chief agreed to sell an area of

Lapowinsa, by Gustavus Hesselius, 1735 *The Historical Society of Pennsylvania*

land bounded by a one and a half day's walk. This was a standard measurement to the Indians, and it meant about twenty miles. But on the appointed day the colonists sent runners down a path already secretly cut in the forest, and covered twice the distance. In Hesselius's portrait of Lapowinsa, we see a face too noble to expect such a trick, as in fact he did not. But it shows, too, the sadness of one who knows that the battle is already lost.

John Smibert and Robert Feke

Little-known European painters, often hardly better than amateurs, had come to find their fortune in America. But now Americans were wealthy enough to attract well-known and successful European artists. The first of these to arrive was John Smibert. Smibert was born in Edinburgh in 1688, the son of a dyer. With great difficulty he

Catherine Hendrickson, by an unknown artist, 1770   *National Gallery of Art, Washington, D.C.*
Edgar William and Bernice Chrysler Garbisch Collection

The Bermuda Group: Dean George Berkeley and his Family, by John Smibert, 1729   *Yale University Art Gallery. Gift of Isaac Lothrop*

Isaac Royall and Family, by Robert Feke, 1741   *Courtesy of the Harvard University Portrait Collection*

worked, first as a house painter and then as a painter of coach doors, toward his goal of becoming a recognized artist in London. This he achieved, but it was not enough. Smibert wanted to be considered the very best painter in London, and he was not. He was described as "a silent, modest man who abhorred the finess of his profession."

One day Smibert received an extraordinary invitation. The well-known philosopher Bishop Berkeley asked him to join a group that was going to the New World to set up a "universal college of the arts and sciences" to teach the Indians of Bermuda. Smibert was the very man to be excited by such an adventure. He sailed with Berkeley and his group, and after four months arrived in Newport in 1729. Here plans fell through. Berkeley ran out of money, and as none arrived from England, he was unable to set up his school. Nothing daunted, Smibert traveled to Boston, then a city the size of his native Edinburgh. He was by far the best artist that had ever come to America, and he enjoyed an instant success. Smibert, the dark and dour Scot, married a beautiful Boston heiress, and his studio became a meeting place. When it was opened in 1730, he held the first art exhibition in America, showing his own works, of course.

Let us look at Smibert's painting of Bishop Berkeley and the group with which he came to America (page 47). The Bishop stands to the right, deep in thought, his eyes to heaven. Seated at the table are his wife, holding their son, Henry, and her sister. The man taking dictation from the Bishop is a member of the group, Richard Dalton, while another member, John James, stands behind the women. On the far left, behind his own nephew, Dr. Thomas Moffat, stands the artist himself, with long, pointed nose and dark eyes, his features set and deadly serious. This is a huge painting—all eight figures are life size. And although he had just arrived, Smibert already painted in the American manner. Every face is a real one—the plain child, the worried Mr. James, the cheerless artist himself. The setting alone is unreal. The sitters are grouped around a table which is covered with a turkey-work rug and stands in the open air, surrounded by a paradise of trees. But the people themselves seem alive, crisscrossing the canvas with gestures and glances. They are adventurers, everyone willing to make sacrifices for their ideals.

Why is the work of John Smibert so important to us? Because he was the first highly trained artist to work in America, and because he was important to the first truly great artist born in America, Robert Feke.

Robert Feke is a man of mystery. We know practically nothing about him. One day in 1741 he walked into Smibert's studio. The stranger had "exactly the phiz [short for physiognomy, or physical appearance] of a painter, having a long, pale face; sharp nose; large eyes with which he looked upon you steadfastly; long, curled black hair; a delicate white hand; and long fingers." Where did he come from? No one knows. Legend has it that he was born in Oyster Bay, Long Island. He seems at one time to have been a seaman, and when he first met Smibert he was already an artist. Where or how did he study? That is another mystery. It is even possible that, as a sailor, he picked up some skills in England. One of his earliest pictures, his portrait of *Isaac Royall and Family* (page 47), tells us two things. First, he was much impressed by Smibert's painting of the Berkley group. If we compare the two, we will see that Feke has copied the composition, with a few changes, adding one woman and leaving out all men except Isaac Royall, who stands in the place of Bishop Berkeley. The picture tells us another astonishing fact: Robert Feke was already the greatest painter in America. How much less crowded, more gracious, and relaxed Feke's painting is. The anatomy of the figures is more correct, their gestures more natural. The color is softer and more pleasing. How Feke learned to paint this way remains as much a mystery as his fate.

Feke painted many portraits between 1741 and 1750, when he was last heard of, living in Philadelphia. And then—nothing more is known. According to a family story, he went to Bermuda for his health, but there is no record that he was ever there. Feke was America's first truly great native-born artist, and we do not even know when or where he died.

Art in the South

Something is missing in our story. We have spoken of the arts and crafts in the cities and towns and even the back country of the northern and central colonies, but what was happening in the South? Life in the southern colonies was a very different matter. There were no cities and only a few towns, the largest of which was Charleston. There were few small farms. The land was divided into great plantations, each one a town in itself. Each had its own wharf, on the coast or on a river, from which boats could sail directly to England. And because there were no towns, there were no free craftsmen. The planters shipped their produce—tobacco, rice, or indigo—directly to England and received in return fine furniture, china, silver, and everything they needed for their plantation houses. Their art came straight from London. Even

Mrs. Abraham White and Daughter Rose, by Joshua Johnston, c. 1810 *Chrysler Museum at Norfolk. Gift of Col. Edgar and Bernice Chrysler Garbisch*

Self-Portrait, attributed to Joshua Johnston, early 19th century *Collection of Edgar William and Bernice Chrysler Garbisch*

George Washington ordered "one neat landskip three feet by 21½ inches" from London. If a planter could not go to London for his portrait, the picture would be painted there all the same, *from a written description of his face.*

On the plantations, the slaves were the craftsmen, making everything necessary that could not be easily imported from England. And we know, too, that some of them became artists as well. A Boston newspaper advertised the work of a black "whose extraordinary genius has been assisted by the best masters in London." Joshua Johnston of Baltimore (active 1796–1824) showed such talent that, if he was not born free, he was given his freedom. Although we know little about his life, he is listed in Baltimore as a registered painter, and we can tell from his self-portrait that he was a successful one. He is elegantly dressed in the fashion of his day. His painting of *Mrs. Abraham White and Daughter Rose* must have been a perfect likeness of the narrow-featured young Baltimore mother in her velvets and delicately painted laces. Once we have seen the portrait, we would recognize her face anywhere. Mrs. White's family would have something far more

49

real to remember her by than the friends and relatives of those whose portraits were painted by mail from England.

Genre Painting

Another question might come to mind. Did colonial artists paint nothing but portraits? We know from records such as wills that they certainly did. We read of still lifes, landscapes and seascapes, paintings of historical and religious subjects, and "genre" scenes of everyday life. Very few of these are left. The painting *Christ Talketh with a Woman of Samaria* was painted by an artist of the Hudson River valley. We see Christ in the colonial countryside, speaking to the woman before

Christ Talketh with a Woman of Samaria, by an unknown artist, c. 1710   *National Gallery of Art, Washington, D.C. Gift of Edgar William and Bernice Chrysler Garbisch*

Sea Captains Carousing in Surinam, by John Greenwood, c. 1758 *The St. Louis Art Museum*

a well, painted with such poor perspective that it seems to be tipping over. The woman is surprised that he knows the details of her life, and she listens to his words. Probably the artist was little more than a sign painter, but the picture was meant to teach a lesson in religion. There were doubtless many such.

John Greenwood's painting, on the other hand, shows exactly how lively the colonists could be. It is entitled *Sea Captains Carousing in Surinam,* but in fact it is a picture of the worthy citizens of Newport misbehaving. It was painted on six feet of bed ticking, and all the "carousers" have had too much to drink. The man in the center, who has fallen asleep at the table, was one of the city's most respected merchants. A prominent sea captain is shown vomiting into his pocket while his jacket tails catch fire. The future Commander-in-Chief of the Continental navy holds up a toast to two other prominent citizens who dance. The future Governor of Rhode Island is chatting away at the table, while the artist himself staggers out the door.

Such paintings are fascinating because they tell us what life in the colonies was really like. Why have we so many portraits left, but so few genre paintings? The explanation is easy. For reasons we shall see, most colonial paintings quickly went out of style. They were taken down from walls and stored in attics as more fashionable pictures took their place. Years later, they were found peeling and often torn, so there seemed little reason to restore or keep them. If the frame was still good, it was placed around a new painting. Only a few, mostly pictures of towns or colleges, were kept for historical or sentimental reasons. But this was never true of portraits. No matter how old-fashioned the painting, an ancestor on the wall meant that the family had a prosperous history. Grandfather's silks and laces were a matter of pride, no matter how badly painted. Portraits were the family's totem pole.

4

FOUR ARTISTS OF THE AMERICAN REVOLUTION

Revolutionaries in Art

By the middle of the eighteenth century, it was clear that the American colonies could no longer be ruled by men in London, almost a month's journey away. These men did not know the problems of the colonists, and governed in their own interest. Squabbles arose, especially over the payment of taxes to a government in which the colonists had no voice. From the beginning the colonies were settled by people who sought freedom from the powers of Europe, and now the break could no longer be delayed.

The generation of the Revolution was a generation of revolutionaries in art as well. For the first time, native-born artists in the colonies were as important as European artists and were not imitators of European styles, but leaders.

The lives of four of the greatest of these —Benjamin West (1738–1820), John Singleton Copley (1738–1815), Charles Willson Peale (1741–1827), and Gilbert Stuart (1755–1828) — are adventures worth the telling.

Benjamin West

Benjamin West was brought up in the little town of Springfield, Pennsylvania, on the very edge of the frontier, the son of a Quaker tinsmith turned innkeeper. Young Benjamin was one of ten children.

Springfield was not the kind of town where much thought was devoted to art. In fact, it consisted of no more than a few small houses and cabins, with a stockade hastily put up as a defense against Indians. Probably not a single *picture* decorated a wall in the entire town, and few of its inhabitants had ever seen one. Still, young Benjamin West felt he must paint. He had never seen a paint brush, but a visiting friend had described one. We are told that Benjamin promptly made a brush of his own, using the nearest thing at hand—the fur from a cat's tail. What did he use for paint? Although the frontiersmen did not realize it, they were surrounded by expert mixers of color. Many years later, Benjamin West, then an old man and a revered artist, told how the Indians taught him to make paints from natural earths. His first paintings would not have seemed very exciting to us, but so impressed were the villagers by what they saw that they banded together to send their local genius to Philadelphia for a brief visit. There he was introduced to a professional artist, William Williams.

Benjamin's visit to William Williams was the great adventure of his young life. Williams filled the boy's ears with tales of his travels and his eyes with paintings such as he had never imagined. While young West sat in a corner of the studio, listening intently, Williams told him the extraordinary story of his life: how he, like Benjamin, had wanted to be a painter as a boy but was forced by poverty to become a sailor. He told how he was shipwrecked in Central America and how he found a cave in which to live, how he met an Indian family that cared for him and taught him their language. He described his adventures in the jungle in every detail, from the shape of the seacoast to the appearance of a flock of flamingos that looked like a band of redcoats. And he told Benjamin how he eventually developed his talent for painting and made Philadelphia his home.

Slowly, laboriously, over the next few years young West learned to paint. As soon as he was old enough to leave his frontier home for good, the ambitious West returned to Philadelphia where he attended the local college and where he could study, firsthand, the finest paintings then in America. At eighteen he painted *Sarah Ursula Rose* (page 54). The figure is nicely rounded, and she wears a splendid satin dress, but there could be no bones beneath her shapeless flesh. Within two years these problems were solved. At twenty, West was a fine portraitist. But this was not enough. He had seen a Spanish painting, captured with a treasure ship, that made him feel that he must go to Europe to study. He had no money, but the merchants of Philadelphia were as anxious to help the young artist as the villagers of Springfield had been. As one Philadelphian put it, "It is a pity such a genius should be cramped for want of a little cash."

At the age of twenty-one West sailed for

Self-Portrait, by Benjamin West, c. 1770 *National Gallery of Art, Washington, D.C. Andrew W. Mellon Collection*

Italy, where he studied the works of the great painters of the Italian Renaissance. A self-portrait shows him to have been a slender, dark, and handsome young man, and he quickly made many friends. Six years later, he decided it was time to return home. His father, to whom "home" had always been England, begged him to pay a visit to London. This he did, and found the English so hospitable that he decided to stay for a while.

But West's short stay in London became a longer and longer one. He began to paint, and was immediately successful. In fact, his success was overwhelming. Two years later he decided that he must return to America for a visit, and to marry his childhood sweetheart, Elizabeth Shewell of Philadelphia. But friends convinced him that it would be a mistake to leave at the height of his new found fame, so he arranged for his father to bring Elizabeth to London. The older West had yearned to return to England for many years, but he found London so changed that he was happy enough to go back to the colonies. Poor Elizabeth remained as West's faithful wife for

Sarah Ursula Rose, by Benjamin West, 1756   *The Metropolitan Museum of Art. Gift of Edgar William and Bernice Chrysler Garbisch, 1964*

fifty years, so homesick for Philadelphia that she tried to grow corn in the cloudy damp of her English greenhouse. Neither she nor her husband ever returned to America.

What kind of painting was it that thrilled Londoners and made the handsome young American so admired? West's portrait of *Colonel Guy Johnson* will give us some idea. Johnson was the first Superintendent of Indian Affairs. He was an Englishman, and West painted his portrait in London in 1776, although the American wilderness appears in the background. Colonel Johnson is clearly a man who has struck out into the wilderness and come to know the Indians well. Beside him stands a noble Indian chieftain, who meaningfully holds a peace pipe to which he points. He appears dressed as West knew the Indians to dress in his childhood. Johnson was actu-

Colonel Guy Johnson, by Benjamin West, 1776
National Gallery of Art, Washington, D.C.
Andrew W. Mellon Collection

The Death of Wolfe, by Benjamin West, 1770   *The National Gallery of Canada, Ottawa. Gift of the Duke of Westminster, 1918*

ally accompanied to London by his secretary and close friend, Chief Thayenda-negea of the Mohawks, known to the English as Captain Joseph Brant. For almost the first time, Europeans could have some idea of how native Americans really looked. Colonel Johnson himself wears quillwork moccasins. His red military uniform is casually open and trimmed with beadwork, and he wears an Indian cape. For the Londoners who crowded West's studio, all these details were fascinating.

But portraits were not West's true interest. Ever since the moment in his childhood when William Williams had lent him a book on what was called the "grand manner" in painting, West had wanted to paint huge and dramatic canvases of historical subjects. These were thought to be the most serious, the highest form of art. When he unveiled his painting of *The Death of Wolfe,* the people who saw it were astonished. West had chosen a tense moment during the French and Indian Wars and painted it dramatically. All eyes are drawn to the dying General Wolfe, who

took the French General Montcalm by surprise and won the siege of Quebec. Other figures are grouped about, showing expressions of care, grief, and amazement. But what seemed most strange to the London public was the fact that the figures are all dressed in precisely the clothing they would have worn—rumpled and tattered British uniforms. Their surprise may seem strange to us, but any other artist of West's day would have painted such a historical moment in Roman dress, with the hero in the breastplate and plumed helmet of a Roman general. That West should paint Wolfe and his soldiers in the uniform of the British army, and that he should have added, not the figure of a classical god, but an American Indian, was revolutionary. West, always pennywise, charged admission to view the new painting, which was also something that had never been done before.

This love of realism that West showed in his painting of *The Death of Wolfe* appears over and over in American art. We saw it in the stern and unusual faces of the early portraits—Mrs. Freake, Anne Pollard, Mr. Van Vechten, and Mr. Willson—and we will see it often again. It is said that when West painted *The Battle of La Hogue* (page 58), realistically set in the dress of an earlier century, an admiral of the Royal Navy ordered several ships to maneuver in false action and fire their guns, so that West could study the appearance of smoke during a naval encounter.

All his life, West was a kind, simple, and natural man. Leigh Hunt, the English author, described him: "He was a man with regular, mild features; and, though of Quaker origin, had the look of what he was, a painter to a court. . . . Yet this man, so well bred, so indisputably clever in his art, had received so careless, or so homely an education when a boy, that he could hardly read. He pronounced . . . *haive* for *have*." West was always a son of the frontier, and he never forgot that he was an American. He welcomed young Americans to his studio and was the inspiration and teacher of the first great generation of American painters. For half a century, every promising young artist in America made his way to London to study with West, and each brought something of West back to America.

West spent the years of the American Revolution in England. What were his feelings? Although he was a close friend of the King, his sympathies were always with the Americans. This seemed to make little difference to the British. Such was his success that when Sir Joshua Reynolds, the great English painter and a founder of the Royal Academy, died in 1792, West became its next president. The frontier boy who had never seen a painting and had made a brush from a cat's tail became the most highly honored painter in England.

One day in 1805 the elderly West paid a visit to a friend, Thomas Eagles. As he waited for his host, he picked up a finely bound book and casually began to read. It told of a young sailor shipwrecked in Central America, of the cave where he made a home, of flamingos that looked like a company of redcoats. . . . "Where did you get this book?" West demanded to know. His friend explained that the manuscript had been left to him in the will of a beggar for whom he arranged a place in the poorhouse. "My two sons were killed at Bunker Hill," the beggar had told him. "I have been a painter, but am now old and alone." Tears came into West's eyes as he remembered the thrills of his boyhood. "I know the man too," said West, "and what is more extraordinary, had it not been for him, I should never have been a painter." Poor William Williams went to a pauper's grave, but the story of the adventures of his youth became the success of London and was admired by Lord Byron himself. His pupil, Benjamin West, like the great men of England, was carried to his rest from Saint Paul's Cathedral. He died a man who was happy, as Leigh Hunt said, "because he thought himself immortal."

John Singleton Copley

When John Singleton Copley was thirteen, tragedy struck his family. His stepfather, who had taught him to draw and paint, died. Young Copley already knew that he wanted to be an artist. Moreover, he was the only man in the family, and he had a mother and a new baby brother to support. Carefully, with tiny strokes of his brush, the boy copied first Smibert and Feke, and then whatever artists were popular in his home town of Boston at the time. By the age of eighteen he was a popular young artist who could turn out a portrait as well as anyone in the colonies. At twenty, Copley could paint a better portrait than any artist in America. So it was that like Benjamin West who painted landscapes when he had never seen one, Copley was painting portraits greater than any he had seen. But this was not enough. Copley still wanted to improve his art. It is thought that all artists are taught by the works of artists who went before them, but Copley was taught by the appearance of nature itself. He tried, with every small stroke of the brush, to capture the reality of what he saw.

Let us look at Copley's portrait of Epes Sargent, a respected merchant of Salem, Massachusetts (page 59). His sitter is a man heavy with age, and Copley has done nothing to hide the fact.

Epes Sargent, by John Singleton Copley, c. 1760   *National Gallery of Art, Washington, D.C.*
Gift of the Avalon Foundation

The Battle of La Hogue, by Benjamin West, 1778   *National Gallery of Art, Washington, D.C.*
Andrew W. Mellon Fund

Paul Revere, by John Singleton Copley, c. 1768–70
*Courtesy, Museum of Fine Arts, Boston. Gift of
Joseph W., William B., and Edward H. R. Revere*

He has painted old age as never before in America
—the thin lips, the dry skin, and the cheeks pink
with broken blood vessels, are all here. Not only
is the face realistic, but the figure is also, the heavy
body and hands, not soft and delicate, but hard
and deeply wrinkled with age. Finally, something
in the smile of the sitter tells us of the shrewd good
humor of the man himself. At twenty-two, Copley
was already perhaps one of the finest portraitists
in the world, but of course there was no way that
he could know it.

Realism to Copley meant not only painting
an **exact** likeness, the perfect texture of cloth,
hair, and flesh. It also meant painting the Boston
silversmith Paul Revere in his shirtsleeves at his
workbench, with the tools of his trade around
him. In England, and in America until this time,
any man who could afford the price of a portrait
could also afford a fine coat, and would most
certainly pose wearing it. His portrait was meant
to show the sitter's rank in society. But as often
as possible Copley's portraits showed, not rank,
but the man himself. It was Paul Revere, the
artist and craftsman who made the magnificent
tankard shown earlier, who flung himself on his
horse the night of April 18, 1775. Riding hard,
he helped to warn the farmers of Concord and
Lexington that a thousand British troops were

coming to raid their hidden supplies. In the painting we can see the stubborn, blunt features of the
patriot who was said to be "cool in thought,
ardent in action." The best of Feke's portraits
could not be compared to this.

When he was not working on an important
commission, Copley enjoyed painting his young
half-brother, Henry Pelham. One such picture
was to be among the most important paintings in
Copley's career. A friend, a sea captain by trade,
took such a liking to a portrait entitled *Boy with
Squirrel* that he insisted on carrying it off with him
to England for exhibition at the Society of Artists
(later the Royal Academy) . It caused a sensation.
Both Sir Joshua Reynolds and Benjamin West,
already famous in London, were amazed that any
artist who had never left the colonies, and had
never studied the masterpieces of Europe, could
create such a painting. Copley was immediately
voted a member of the Society of Artists. Reynolds
wrote, "If you are capable of producing such a
piece by the efforts of your own genius, with the
advantages of example and instruction you would
have in Europe you would be a valuable acquisi-
tion to the art and one of the first painters in the
world." *One of the first painters in the world.*
What these words must have meant to Copley,
who could only imagine the works of the world's
greatest artists, and the great cities of Europe. He
was in a quandary. Should he go to Europe? Should
he leave his home, his friends, his successful career
and comfortable livelihood as Boston's first
painter? Or should he stay and miss forever his
chance, perhaps, to be the world's greatest artist?
He was still torn by these questions when fate
stepped in.

At the age of thirty-one, Copley married
Susanna Clarke (whom he called "Sukey") , the
daughter of Richard Clarke, one of the wealthiest
merchants in Boston. The date was 1769, and the
Revolution was in the making. The city of Boston
was divided. Copley, a shy and peace-loving man,
would not take sides. As we have seen, many of
his friends were patriots. His father-in-law was
a Tory. In 1773 it so happened that Richard
Clarke received a very important shipment of tea.
In fact, this was the tea that so infuriated the

patriots—untaxed British tea that would undersell what American merchants, whose tea was taxed, could provide. The patriots demanded that Clarke send it back, an act that was illegal in the eyes of the British and would cost Clarke his ships. Clarke fled the city. Copley ran back and forth from one party to the other, trying to soothe tempers, trying to stop the revolution in its tracks. He pleaded with a howling mob at a town meeting, and took their terms to the merchants. He thought he had succeeded. Then, on the night of December 16, a hundred and fifty patriots, dressed as "Mohawks," boarded the ships and dumped the tea in the harbor. The "Boston Tea Party" was one of the first acts of open rebellion against the British. Poor Copley. To the patriots he was a Tory, and to the Tories he appeared a friend of the patriots. Clearly, he could not stay in Boston. This was the moment to do what he had really wanted to do. He sailed for Europe in June of 1774. He left his wife and young children behind—war was far off, he thought.

When war broke out, Copley was in Italy. He rushed to London in hope of arranging the rescue of his wife and children, but they had already arrived in England. That very year, he painted a portrait of his family that is one of the most winning, lively, and true portraits of a family group ever painted (page 62). We all know that when such a group poses for its picture, even a photograph, the adults will try to remain dignified, but the children will soon be "out of control." In the painting, the Copley family has given up the almost hopeless struggle. Compared with the prettily posed portraits of children by other artists of Copley's day, this is amazing realism. On the right, Copley's son, John Singleton Copley, Jr., and daughter Mary are climbing all over their mother. Little John is pulling his mother's head down in an effort to kiss her. The children have tossed a doll and a hat on the floor. On the left, Copley's father-in-law, Richard Clarke, holds the youngest child, Susanna, who is just at the age when children pull apart the clothing of the people on whose laps they sit—and Susanna is no exception. Her grandfather is pretending not to notice, but the expression on his face betrays him.

It does not surprise us that the Revolutionaries dumped his tea. Of the children, only the oldest daughter, Elizabeth, seems to know or care that she is posing for a picture. She stands right in the middle, trying hard to pose prettily and look directly at the artist. Copley has placed a portrait of himself behind the group, quiet and shy man that he was, in order to complete the family. Only the setting is unreal. The family's rugs and furniture seem to have been hauled out-of-doors. Behind them is a landscape—and it does not look like England. It looks like the wilderness of America.

Did Copley learn from the art of Europe and become one of the first painters in the world? The answer is disappointing. Copley was already one of the world's first portraitists, although he himself did not realize it, and the art of Europe proved to be a poorer teacher than nature itself, back in Boston.

Benjamin West, of course, welcomed young Copley to his studio. Copley admired West, and decided that he, too, would give up portraiture for more "important" historical painting in the grand manner. One of the first he attempted was *Watson and the Shark* (page 63). Sir Brook Watson, a wealthy London merchant and friend of Copley's, had started life as a poor orphan, and had risen to become Lord Mayor of London. When he was a boy, like so many men of the eighteenth century who rose from poverty to wealth, he went to sea. One day when he was fourteen, while swimming in the harbor of Havana, he was attacked by a shark that bit off part of his leg. Copley has created a great action painting. In the damp heat of Havana sailors from the nearby British fleet have come to rescue the boy from the lunging shark. Here is Copley's realism at its best, and the picture fills us with the terror of the moment. The painting was exhibited at the Royal Academy and made Copley famous overnight.

But, in a way, success brought Copley failure. Copley was a far greater portraitist than West had ever been, and now he turned from portraiture to history painting. But Copley's talent was for painting exactly what he saw before him. His history paintings, except for *Watson and the Shark,* lacked the great realism of his portraits.

The Copley Family, by John Singleton Copley, c. 1776   *National Gallery of Art, Washington, D. C.*
Andrew W. Mellon Fund

Watson and the Shark, by John Singleton Copley, 1778   *National Gallery of Art, Washington, D.C.*
Ferdinand Lammot Belin Fund

In England he was influenced by the stylish painting around him, and even the portraits he painted while there seem weak and artificial.

Meanwhile, in America, a new country had been born. Copley should have been its master painter, but in the confusion of the Revolution he found himself on the wrong side. He must have yearned for the home he would never see again. In 1782 he was painting the portrait of an American merchant, Elkanah Watson, in which one of the gentleman's ships appeared in the background. On December 5 the two men went to the House of Lords to hear the recognition of the independence of the United States. According to Watson, they returned to the studio and Copley, "with a bold hand, a master's touch, and I believe an American heart . . . attached to the ship the Stars and Stripes."

Copley lived on in London, successful but sour and embittered. He even fought with West —so nastily that when the King was asked to decide the matter, he said he wished the Devil would take them both. Copley died at the age of seventy-seven, without ever returning to his native Boston.

The Artist in his Museum, by Charles Willson Peale, 1822 *Courtesy of the Pennsylvania Academy of the Fine Arts. Joseph and Sarah Harrison Collection, 1878*

Charles Willson Peale

After Copley left Boston in 1774, the honor of being the colonies' first painter fell to a man only a few years younger, Charles Willson Peale, one of the most extraordinary men in the history of American art. Peale was a good, solid artist, one who had learned to draw well and managed his colors carefully. Like so many painters, he came from a simple family. His father was a convict, condemned for embezzlement and forgery, who chose deportation to America as preferable to the gallows. Young Charles started life as a saddler, but managed to study painting with Gustavus Hesselius, and even with West in London. Peale was an out-and-out patriot. He was a member of the Pennsylvania Assembly and one of Washington's officers. All during the campaigns, during the bitter winter at Valley Forge when all hands froze, and the dank, hot summers, Peale was busy, sketching and painting. One fellow soldier wrote, "He fit [fought] and painted, painted and fit." He painted the portraits of all the great men of the Revolution, soldiers and statesmen alike.

Charles Willson Peale, then, was a painter and a patriot. But in what way was he extraordinary? He was unusual in that, like Leonardo da Vinci, the great artist and scientist of the Renaissance, he was interested in all arts, all crafts, and all of nature. With tremendous energy he set about to learn all there was to know about music, carving, engraving, brass and plaster casting, silversmithing, taxidermy, clock and watch repair, and even dentistry (he invented porcelain false teeth). And he was interested in soldiery and politics. Moreover, he set out to bring learning, and an interest in science, to the nation. In 1786 he established the first museum deserving the name in America. It was situated in Philadelphia, where he went to live, and it was eventually moved to Independence Hall. This was not simply a museum of works of art, but of natural history as well. Peale was at heart a scientist, and to him art was itself a kind of science—the science of representing visual images on a flat surface. The main purpose of art, Peale felt, was to record facts. In Peale's own matter-of-fact self-portrait, he exhibits his museum with some pride. It was divided into sections: America's wildlife (mounted animals before painted backdrops, surrounded by the vegetation in which they lived), America's history (Peale's collection of portraits of great Revolutionary leaders), and America's past (including Indian relics and fossils). In painting himself and his museum, Peale has added to the picture a wild turkey, the symbol of the new country.

Peale had three wives and no less than seventeen children. He named many of them after the great painters of the past: Raphaelle, Titian, Rembrandt, Rubens, and Van Dyck. The girls were named after women artists: Angelica Kauffman, Sophonisba Angusciola, and Rosalba Carriera. All were encouraged to take an interest in all the arts and all the sciences. *Exhuming the First American Mastodon* is a family portrait of a typical Peale outing. The first mastodon had been discovered, and the Peale family were out toiling in the mud, digging and assembling bones for the museum.

Charles Willson Peale's energies never failed. In his seventies he painted a portrait of his brother by lamplight to study the painting of a scene set in darkness, and the self-portrait we have seen was painted when he was eighty-one. He died at the age of eighty-six, while energetically courting a fourth wife.

Charles Willson Peale headed a "dynasty," a vast family of artists and scientists. His brother James, who painted miniatures, had seven children, five of whom were artists. Of the children who struggled through the mud to "exhume the mastodon," several became artists as well. The most successful was Rembrandt Peale, the apple of his father's eye, for whom George Washington posed when young Peale was only seventeen. Rembrandt went to London to study with Benjamin West, and painted many of the great men of his day, including Thomas Jefferson (page 66). Niece Sarah Miriam became the leading portrait painter in Baltimore.

The Peales tried their hand at every type of gadget and invention. Raphaelle toured the country with a "physiognotrace," a machine that traced the shadow of a profile on paper. He devised ways of protecting a ship's bottom, "making putrid water sweet," and even wrote a *Theory of the Universe.* Raphaelle was also an artist. He was the finest still-life painter of his day. His picture en-

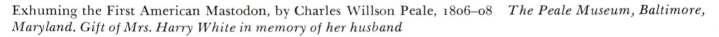

Exhuming the First American Mastodon, by Charles Willson Peale, 1806–08   *The Peale Museum, Baltimore, Maryland. Gift of Mrs. Harry White in memory of her husband*

After the Bath, by Raphaelle Peale, 1823 *Nelson Gallery—Atkins Museum, Kansas City, Missouri*

was an American who said that he had returned from Dublin especially to paint Washington. In fact, he was fleeing prison.

Gilbert Stuart was the son of a poor snuff grinder, employed by none other than the nephew of the artist Smibert. Like West, Copley, and so many others, he was already an artist when still a child. At fourteen, he was painting portraits in his home town of Newport, Rhode Island. His early life was full of adventure. He was discovered by a Scottish painter who took him to work as an apprentice in Edinburgh; but when his teacher died, he had to make his way back to America as a sailor. Three years later, and still impoverished, he again sailed for England, on the day before the Battle of Bunker Hill. Stuart went to study with Benjamin West, and soon was a better portrait painter than his master. By the age of twenty-eight, he was able to set up a studio of his own. All he needed was one stroke of luck. It came one cold day, when a sitter, a Mr. Grant of

titled *After the Bath* is actually a *trompe l'oeil,* a "trick on the eye." It looks like a painting of a nude figure over which a freshly starched white napkin has been hung. The napkin seems so real we almost feel we could pluck it away from the canvas and see the nude (presumably wet) figure underneath.

Raphaelle was a lovable man who joked and drank a great deal, but never enjoyed great success. His last job was to compose love poems for the party cakes of a local bakery. Rembrandt built the first "illuminating gasworks" in Philadelphia, and Titian took to exploring Florida, South America, and the South Seas. Between them, the Peales established museums in Baltimore, New York, and Utica. On their own, the family tried to bring both art and science to the new nation.

Gilbert Stuart

When we think of George Washington, a face appears before our eyes. We have seen it a thousand times over, and almost certainly it is the face of a portrait by Gilbert Stuart. The artist

Thomas Jefferson, by Rembrandt Peale, 1803 *Courtesy of the New-York Historical Society, New York City*

The Skater, by Gilbert Stuart, 1782 *National Gallery of Art, Washington, D.C. Andrew W. Mellon Collection*

George Washington, by Gilbert Stuart, 1795 *National Gallery of Art, Washington, D.C. Andrew W. Mellon Collection*

Mrs. Richard Yates, by Gilbert Stuart *National Gallery of Art, Washington, D.C. Andrew W. Mellon Collection*

Congalton, remarked that it was a better day for skating than for painting. The gentlemen took off for a lake in the park, and the result was Stuart's painting *The Skater*, his portrait of Mr. Grant on the ice. It was such a success that Stuart's reputation was made, and he was flooded with commissions.

Here we come to a weakness in Gilbert Stuart's character that was unlucky for him, but lucky for his native land. He was a great success in London, and money poured in. But it was never enough. He loved to spend it, and he lived in splendor. He was such a dandy that he was better dressed than the Prince of Wales (the heir to the throne); and he kept a French cook to entertain his friends at nightly parties. In the eighteenth century, debtors were put in prison, which is exactly where Stuart found himself, despite his dashing charm. He soon escaped to Dublin where for a time all went well. He was again a success, but again in debt, and again in flight, this time back to America.

Once home, he was immediately accepted

as the finest painter in the country. He said he had returned to America because of his love of liberty, and because he wanted to paint Washington. When he heard this, Sir Thomas Laurence, the great English portraitist, snapped, "I knew Stuart well, and I believe the real cause of his leaving England was his having become tired of the inside of some of our prisons." "Well then," said Lord Holland, "after all, it was his love of freedom that took him to America."

In any case, and for whatever reason, Stuart did paint Washington—two times from life and over and over again in copies of his original portraits. Copley had painted slowly, carefully; but Stuart could capture a likeness in a few quick strokes. Faces interested him more than anything else, and at times he would leave the rest of the canvas blank. Flesh, he said, "is like no other substance under heaven. It has all the gaiety of a silk-mercer's shop without its gaudiness of gloss, and all the soberness of old mahogany without its sadness." He could suggest it to the eye with the greatest of ease, and to bring out the character beneath he would chat and joke endlessly with his sitters. In his later years he told a friend how embarrassed he was when he first painted Washington, and how difficult it was to make him "speak on light subjects." Stuart eventually managed to tell a joke that made Washington laugh, but the impression Washington first made on the artist is the one we get from the picture—a man above the reality of everyday life, a figure of heroic majesty. We know from Washington's letters that he was a warm, humorous, and very real person. Were the Stuart portraits true likenesses? We know that Washington thought them to be, but his wife felt they were not—to her

they did not suggest his impressive height, or his physical strength.

Stuart's portraits of Washington give us the image all Americans have in their hearts of the lofty ruler. We must not think, however, that this was usual with Stuart's portraits. A witty man himself, Stuart usually brought out the wit in his sitters, like *Mrs. Richard Yates* (page 67), whom he has caught at her needlework. We can tell that the artist and the stern but cross-eyed lady have been gossiping.

As we have seen, America's artists played different roles in the Revolution. Charles Willson Peale and Paul Revere were patriots, willing to fight for their country to the last breath. Benjamin West and Gilbert Stuart were not even present. Copley ended up on the British side with his crabbed father-in-law. But this does not matter. All were working, in one way or another, to give America an art that the country could call its own, and of which it could be proud. Most had begun in impoverished boyhoods and worked against all odds to create something important where little had been before. And they succeeded. From the point of view of art they were, like Washington, Adams, Hancock, and the others, founders of a new nation. On the outbreak of the Revolution Copley wrote: "Poor America. . . . Yet certain I am she will finally emerge from her present calamity and become a mighty empire. And it is a pleasing reflection that I shall stand among the first of the artists that shall have led the country to the knowledge and cultivation of the Fine Arts, happy in the pleasing reflection that they will one day shine with a luster not inferior to what they have done in Greece and Rome."

5

THE NINETEENTH CENTURY

The Classical Revival

Among his many interests, Thomas Jefferson was a gentleman architect. He wanted to build a new country, not only politically, but also in stone. Clearly, the great houses of England could no longer serve as models. The new country was to be the first true republic since the early days of Rome and Greece, and so he felt that the architecture of the republic must be the "Classical" architecture of ancient Greece and Rome. We can see it clearly in the Capitol Jefferson designed for his home state, Virginia (page 70), inspired by the Roman temple at Nîmes, which he had seen in France. The columns and the triangular pediment they support are not simply a small decoration, as they are at Mount Vernon. Here the entire building, in its measurements and proportions, is as close as possible to the great buildings of ancient times. When he designed the University of Virginia and his own home, Monticello, Jefferson combined this classic portico and a rotunda plan (for a cir-

cular building with a dome) taken from ancient Rome, with the good red brick of Virginia. Most important, as Secretary of State and as President, Jefferson worked with the Frenchman, Major Pierre Charles L'Enfant, and other engineers and architects, on the plans for the country's new capital at Washington. He envisioned it, as it became, a city of classic monuments. This, then, was the architecture of the American Revolution. As the spirit of the Revolution and the return to "Republican" government spread throughout the West, so did architectural design of ancient Greece and Rome.

With the Louisiana Purchase in 1803, the United States reached as far as the Rocky Mountains, and the new country prospered as never before. Only in the years of the War of 1812 did the country fail to grow. By 1820, New York alone had a population of one hundred and twenty-three thousand, and no less than twenty news-

The Capitol, Richmond, Virginia, designed by Thomas Jefferson (with assistance of Charles-Louis Clerisseau),
1798 *Courtesy, The National Trust for Historic Preservation*

papers. It was a new city. No more than five hundred houses remained that had been standing in 1776. In 1825 the Erie Canal opened a shipping route to the West. When Washington's comrade, the Marquis de Lafayette, returned to America for the first time in the fifty years since the Revolution, he was confused to find himself greeted by a vast crowd, made up of immigrants from almost every race and nation on earth, who were swiftly becoming one nation. He was entertained at receptions, dinners, and balls that were very different from his memories of Washington's day. He looked at the women dazzlingly dressed in the latest fashion and covered with jewels, and found himself surrounded by wealth and elegance. Remembering simple citizens in their leather aprons, like Paul Revere, as Copley painted him, Lafayette looked about and asked, "But where are *the people?*"

The wealthy built splendid homes in the style of the Classical Revival. The earlier "Federal"

style, in which classical motifs could be used on a less grand scale and adapted to simpler houses, became the fashion for smaller but comfortable homes throughout America. Within such a house, one might find graceful furniture designed along Greek (or Roman) lines by French cabinetmakers who brought the fashion from the France of Napoleon. This was the style of much of the furniture made by America's first truly famous cabinetmaker, Duncan Phyfe (1768–1854), the son of a Scottish widow, who brought her children to settle in New York State shortly after the Revolution. Phyfe based the sofa shown here on the couches on which the Romans reclined.

We have been speaking of American artists of every type, from painters to silversmiths and cabinetmakers, but we have said little about American sculpture. The truth is that until the nineteenth century there were few important American sculptors. It was not until America had a revolution to commemorate that the country

70

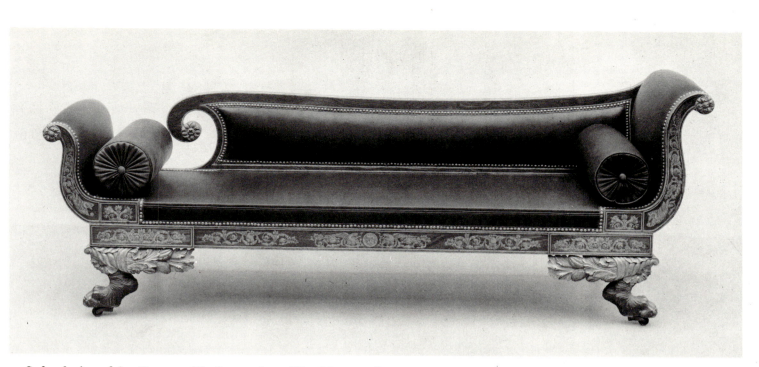

Sofa, designed by Duncan Phyfe, c. 1815   *The Metropolitan Museum of Art. Gift of Mrs. Bayard Verplanck, 1940*

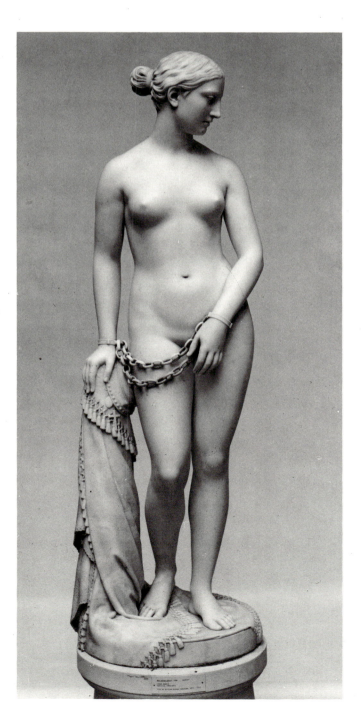

stood in need of monuments, or sculptors to decorate them with splendid figures. When the Revolution was over, American artists were unprepared. Searching for a sculptor to create a figure of Washington for the new State Capitol at Richmond, Virginia, Jefferson was forced to call on a Frenchman, Jean Antoine Houdon. A few years later, in 1805, two sculptors were born who would one day achieve international fame: Hiram Powers (1805–1873) and Horatio Greenough (1805–1852). Both chose as their model the clean lines, eternal quiet, and perfect beauty of the statuary of the Golden Age of Greece. Hiram Powers' *The Greek Slave* was hailed as one of the century's great achievements in art when it was first seen by the public in 1851. The figure has the straight nose, even features, and perfect proportions of Greek statuary. Like the statues of Greece's greatest age, it has no blemishes or imperfections. It does not resemble any one individual, but rather portrays the "ideal" of beauty.

Its sculptor was born in Vermont and brought up in Cincinnati; and we should not be surprised to learn that, like many Americans, he had a practical bent. Powers devised a method for laying a transatlantic cable, organized a stock company to bring marble from Carrara, and in his youth had astounded the public at the Western Museum in Cincinnati with the creation of wax-

71

The Greek Slave, by Hiram Powers, 1846   *In the collection of the Corcoran Gallery of Art*

works and life-size mechanical dolls. In his early thirties, Powers traveled to Italy, where he remained for the rest of his life, as successful in Europe as he had been in America.

The first commission ever given to an American sculptor by the United States government went to Horatio Greenough, who was asked to create a colossal statue of Washington for the Rotunda of the Capitol. Greenough chose as his model a statue of the god Zeus by the greatest of all Greek sculptors, Phidias. The work has the solemn grandeur of an eternal figure of power. The twenty-ton statue was hauled with great difficulty, by boat and train, from Italy, where Greenough worked, to the Capitol. There it met with jeers and gasps of horror. The idea of Washington nude to the waist was simply more than the upright representatives of the people could bear. The fact did not seem to disturb

George Washington, by Horatio Greenough, 1832–39 *Courtesy of Smithsonian Institution*

Greenough greatly. A Harvard graduate and scholar, he, like Powers, was already famous in Europe as well as the United States. Both sculptors had settled with their families in Florence. Here they found the marble quarries of Carrara near at hand, and the works of the great sculptors of the Renaissance to be admired and studied daily. Like West's studio in London, the workshops of Powers and Greenough in Florence became a magnet which drew all young American sculptors. Through them the spirit of Greece and Rome was "revived in the woods of America."

The Romantics

The American Revolution was part of a general desire for freedom of every kind that moved across the Western world like a fresh wind at the end of the eighteenth century. Poets, writers, and artists wanted their freedom, too, freedom to escape. This new desire for freedom and escape gave birth to what is called the "Romantic movement."

The early settlers in America wanted to escape a wilderness that frightened them with its strangeness, and to surround themselves with what was most familiar and reminded them of their previous homes. Now, in both Europe and America, the reverse was happening. People wanted to escape the dullness of their everyday lives, of business and the struggle for money and the ugliness of the new industry which was growing up all around them. The Romantics, in their paintings and writings, escaped into the beauty of unspoiled nature, to faraway places and faraway times, and into the strange dreams and visions of the mind. They demanded the freedom to feel things deeply, and to show powerful emotions. The quiet, the cool, hard lines of the "Classical Revival" did not appeal to them.

The first of the American Romantics was Washington Allston (1779–1843). Allston was born on a plantation near Charleston, South Carolina. As a child he loved the ghost stories of the old plantation houses, and the slaves' tales of witches and spirits. Years later, he wrote that in

Elijah in the Desert, by Washington Allston, 1818. *Courtesy, Museum of Fine Arts, Boston. Gift of Mrs. Samuel Hooper and Miss Alice Hooper*

his childhood he felt a strong love "for the wild and marvelous. I delighted in being terrified by the tales of witches and hags . . . and I remember with how much pleasure I recalled these feelings on my return to Carolina; especially on revisiting a gigantic wild grape-vine in the woods, which had been the favorite swing of one of these witches."

After graduating from Harvard, Allston made his way to West's studio in London. From West he learned that sense of drama that was the beginning of Romanticism. Allston's art created a world of the emotions, and of dreams. These were not always pleasant dreams—they could be strange, shadowy, fearful dreams, both mystical and fantastic. In his painting of *Elijah in the Desert,* the prophet is a tiny figure in a vast and terrifying desolation. Our eye is drawn to the twisted and tortured branches of a dead tree. It must remind us of the "Dream Land" of another great Roman-

tic, another southerner who spent his childhood in the shadowy mansions of an old plantation, Edgar Allan Poe:

By a route obscure and lonely,
Haunted by ill angels only,
Where an Eidolon, named NIGHT
On a black throne reigns upright,
I have reached these lands but newly
From an ultimate dim Thule—
From a wild weird clime that lieth, sublime,
Out of SPACE—out of TIME.

Allston painted America's first important landscapes. These were not true depictions of views but landscapes that expressed a mood, a realm of the imagination. In his *Moonlit Landscape* (page 74) , the mood is more gentle, but it is mysterious, and there is a hint of suspense. We see

Moonlit Landscape, by Washington Allston, 1819 *Courtesy, Museum of Fine Arts, Boston. Gift of William Sturgis Bigelow*

figures, but we do not know what they are doing. Is this a secret departure? Allston wrote that he wanted his art to give birth to "a thousand things which the eye cannot see." He wanted to appeal "not to the senses, merely, as some have supposed, but rather through them to that region . . . of the imagination which is supposed to be under the . . . domination of music." He wanted to "catch a poet's dream."

Allston also wanted to escape the century in which he lived. To the Romantics, the greatest dramas were the dramas of the past. Allston planned a great painting of the scene of Belshazzar's feast from the Old Testament. Allston worked on this huge canvas during the last twenty-five years of his life. A sketch for it tells us that his project might have been very successful. But the picture tormented him, and he hid it from human sight as he painted and repainted it. Visitors had to approach it backward, so they would not see it. Finally, Allston blacked out the figure of the King. With that act, he died.

Sad to say, although Allston himself was fairly successful, many similar artists found small market for their works in America. In the eighteenth century paintings by America's great artists, such as Copley, were hidden away in private homes. If one wanted to see the work of an artist, it was necessary to pay a private visit to his studio. Now academies of art appeared in every large city, "unions" of artists who banded together to show their work, and the public was happy to pay to attend their exhibitions. Moreover, a successful large historical painting might tour the country, and farmers and their families would come in their buggies from miles around to see a single picture. In this way Rembrandt Peale's painting entitled *The Court of Death* made no less than $9,000 (then a huge sum) in thirteen months. It showed the innocent representatives of humankind (a young man, a widow, and an orphan) attacked by figures representing War, Conflagration, Famine, Pestilence, Pleasure, Intemperance, Remorse, Suicide, Despair, Fever and Gout, among others, and therefore taught a moral lesson. Still, the success of such a tour was a matter of showmanship. In the nineteenth century—with no movies, radio, or television—a huge painting

Study for Belshazzar's Feast, by Washington Allston, 1817 *Courtesy, Museum of Fine Arts, Boston. Bequest of Ruth Charlotte Dana, the artist's niece*

might be the most exciting spectacle to reach a country town all year. However, the truth was that only large institutions could afford such large pictures, which devoured so much of the artist's time. Most Americans still wanted to own portraits of themselves and their families. This hunger of Americans for portraits was fatal to the career of Allston's pupil, Samuel F. B. Morse.

Samuel Finley Breese Morse (1791–1872) was the son of a Congregational minister, who disapproved of his interest in art. At the age of twenty Morse sailed for London as Allston's student. There he labored to become a painter of historical subjects in the grand manner. He was proud of such paintings as *The Dying Hercules* (page 76), showing the twisting body of Hercules brilliantly lit against darkness, a favorite method of the Romantic painters to create a sense of drama. "I cannot be happy unless I am pursuing the intellectual branch of art," he wrote. "Portraits have none of it; landscape has some of it; but history has it wholly." Unfortunately, upon his return to America, Morse's history painting had little success. The public wanted portraits, and would pay

for nothing else. Morse rebelled: "Never will I degrade myself by making a trade of a profession. If I cannot live a gentleman, I will starve a gentleman." Starving did not turn out to be pleasant.

In the nineteenth century the arts and sciences were not divided as they are now. A well-educated man understood both. An excellent example might be Robert Fulton, the inventor of the steamboat, who began his life as an artist and was a student of Benjamin West. Returning to America with his paintings in 1832, Morse found himself in a shipboard conversation about Michael Faraday's experiments in electricity, a subject that had interested him as an undergraduate at Yale. He turned to it now with greater attention. His loss to art proved a gain for the country when, in 1844, the words "What God hath wrought" were transmitted from Washington to Baltimore by way of Morse's telegraph.

We have said that the Romantics wanted to escape into the realm of nature. It was only as civilization and industry began to devour the countryside that Americans began truly to look at the wilderness that surrounded them and ap-

The Dying Hercules, by Samuel
Finley Breese Morse, 1813
Yale University Art Gallery.
Gift of Rev. E. Goodrich Smith

preciate its vast beauty. For the first time, land-scape painters became artists of importance.

As we have seen, Allston painted landscapes. So did Samuel F. B. Morse and many others. But they felt themselves to be history painters. Their landscapes were minor, less important works. Now, true landscape artists began to appear. Thomas Doughty (1793–1856) began life as a leather merchant in Philadelphia. He was a country man who loved hunting and fishing, and when he began to sell artists' supplies in his shop, he took to experimenting. His experiments resulted in landscapes of such charm that painting became his career. Doughty's *Fanciful Landscape* (page 78) is a Romantic dream, somewhat like Allston's. Ancient ruined castles tower above craggy cliffs, over a meandering stream. All is bathed in the warm light of a late afternoon. In the distance, towering

peaks melt into mists; below, tiny figures walk past crashing waterfalls. These warm lights and deep shadows, these delicate mists, are what gave drama to the Romantics' view of life. Here, all is arranged beauty: the tall trees on the left, and the dark cluster on the right, in their grace form a perfect frame for the glistening dream beyond. This is also a painting of mood, not the mood of dark foreboding we saw in Allston's landscapes, but the mood of the poet's soul "lapped in Elysium." This is not to say that Doughty's scenes were all imaginary. He painted the American wilderness, seen through the eyes of a Romantic poet. But the greatest painter of the wilderness of America was Thomas Cole (1801–1848).

In the early months of 1822 a young man could be seen making his way on foot through the forests between the Ohio frontier and the East

Coast. He traveled with a flute, paints, and canvases on his back. When he arrived in a town, he was prepared to play for his dinner, or to paint the faces of whoever felt in need of a portrait in exchange for whatever they might have on hand to pay. "Without knowledge, without training, it was a life and death struggle with me. But it pleased. . . . I painted the visage of a militia officer. This was my best likeness: I could hardly miss it. 'Twas all nose, and in the background a red battle. This tickled him, and I received a silver watch for my pains." The young man had arrived at seventeen from Lancastershire in England, the son of a family that had met with hard times on both sides of the ocean. He had taught himself to paint, and as he wandered through the woods, he realized that the faces of the hard-bitten settlers were not the subjects that pleased him. Reaching Philadelphia, he was able to see landscapes of Doughty in the Pennsylvania Academy. When, in the course of his wanderings, he arrived at the Catskill Mountains, he realized he must paint the fresh, unspoiled wonders of America's wilderness. He painted three landscapes, which found their way into the window of a framer's shop in New York. There they were discovered, and soon young Cole was known to the patrons and artists of the city. His work was shown on exhibition, and within a year Thomas Cole was a founding member of the National Academy of Design. His art was so new to him that he still felt he had to ask questions: "Can figures appear in a landscape? Must there be a body of water?"

For most of his life Cole lived in the village of Catskill in the heart of his beloved mountains. But he wandered far afield into the wilderness, through sun and storm, west to Niagara Falls, and east as far as the great White Mountains of New Hampshire. He did not create his paintings out-of-doors, but everywhere he went he sketched. He jotted down in words the colors, the appearance of the place, and the sensation it gave him. He felt that "to walk into nature as a poet is a necessary condition of the perfect artist," and, like Allston, he wrote verse. Then, when the scene had seeped into his very soul, he would return home and put it on canvas—never exactly as it was, but as he deeply felt it to be. It was not important that every leaf and bough be painted realistically. He wanted the scene as it would appear in a Romantic reverie: "If imagination is shackled, and nothing is described but what we see, seldom will anything truly great be produced, either in Painting or Poetry." These are the words of a true Romantic.

The inspiration for Cole's Romantic reveries, however, was not some never-never land of ruined castles and snow-white peaks, but the wilderness of America, true enough so that his audience could recognize places they knew and loved. This was the great wilderness only newly opened to Europeans and never before painted. It is the country Washington Irving loved to describe: "rocky precipices mantled with primeval forests; deep gorges walled by beetling cliffs, with torrents tumbling as it were from the sky; the savage glens rarely trodden except by the hunter." This was the wilderness where for two years Thoreau lived when he came to know the birds, the animals, and the fish of Walden Pond. It was the scene of the adventures of James Fenimore Cooper, the forests that Hawkeye and Leatherstocking knew so well. Both the wilderness and the men that wrote about it inspired Cole, who chose some of his paintings as settings for scenes in *The Last of the Mohicans*.

When Cole traveled to Europe, his good friend William Cullen Bryant warned him not to forget America or its beauties:

Lone lakes—savannahs where the bison
    roves—
Rock rich with summer garlands—solemn
    streams—
Skies where the desert Eagle wheels and
    screams—
Spring bloom and autum blaze of boundless
    groves.

Cole did not forget. To him, no landscape in Europe could compare with those of his homeland. On page 79 we see his painting of Crawford Notch in the White Mountains of New Hampshire, an "autumn blaze of boundless groves."

The Notch of the White Mountains (Crawford Notch), by Thomas Cole, 1839   *National Gallery of Art, Washington, D.C. Andrew W. Mellon Fund*

Top: Fanciful Landscape, by Thomas Doughty, 1834   *National Gallery of Art, Washington, D.C. Gift of the Avalon Foundation*

Here in New Hampshire the sugar maples turn the pink and orange of fire in the fall, and the birch a pale yellow; the fir trees remain a dark green. Cole has caught the excitement of the color on a crisp autumn day. And, as always a Romantic, he has given the scene drama. An open space is being cleared of twisted and dead trees. Those that remain create menacing shapes on the right. Above, all is sunny; but an oncoming storm broods over the mountain on the left, and mist is settling in the pass.

Cole did not want to be merely a "painter of leaves." He hoped to paint landscapes that might instruct or help humankind. *The Voyage of Life* (page 82) is a series of "allegorical" paintings, in which figures dramatically personify the stages of human life. In these paintings Cole tried to capture the tenderness of childhood, the glorious hopes of youth, the dangers that lie ahead, and man's final heavenly reward.

Landscape paintings were more popular with nineteenth-century Americans than with any other people in the Western world. The great American wilderness was part of their daily life, something they did not need to study in books to understand. Cole had many followers, several of whom lived, for part or all of their lives, in the area of the Hudson River. For this reason it is said that Cole founded the "Hudson River School" of painting. These were not imitators who followed Cole slavishly, but landscapists with ther own, very personal view of the world.

Jasper Francis Cropsey (1823–1900), for example, was fascinated by nothing so much as the brilliant fall foliage of New York. His painting *Autumn—on the Hudson River* (page 83) captures the dramatic effect of the sun breaking through the storm clouds of an autumn's day. It is interesting to compare Cropsey's delicate autumn with the lush color of Cole's painting of Crawford Notch. We can tell that the last thunder of the dying summer has rumbled through the valley of Irving's "Rip Van Winkle" or "The Legend of Sleepy Hollow."

Asher B. Durand (1796–1886) was five years older than Cole. He was one of those who first discovered Cole's work in a framer's window.

But Durand had spent many years as a successful engraver before he took up landscape painting. When he did, it was with great admiration for Cole. In fact, his painting *Kindred Spirits* depicts Cole and his friend William Cullen Bryant together appreciating the delight of a woodland gorge. Unlike Cole, Durand often painted out-of-doors. He felt that only with the scene in front of him could the painter capture its meaning. He might change a branch or tree in the foreground, but the scene must appear exactly as it was. He advised the young artist to find "the lone and tranquil lakes . . . the unshorn mountains . . . the ocean prairies of the West, and many forms of Nature yet spared from the pollutions of civilization."

John Frederick Kensett, a follower of Durand, was interested, most of all, in capturing on canvas the effects of light, particularly the bright clear light of noon. In the nineteenth century, people did not vacation at the beach as they do today. The shore was often considered desolate. But nowhere is light more brilliant and powerful than by the sea, and it is this light which envelopes Kensett's *Coast Scene with Figures*. The painting is smooth, hard, and clear—we see no brush strokes—and light seems to radiate from the canvas. It is because of this "luminous" light that Kensett and other landcapists like him were later called "luminists."

Thomas Cole had only one true pupil and that was Frederic E. Church (1826–1900). Church is called a member of the "Hudson River School," but he wandered far from New York State. He had the Romantics' yearning for far-away places, and the nineteenth century was the great age of exploration. The explorer Richard Burton stole his way to Mecca disguised as a Circassian, and the reporter Henry Morton Stanley made his adventurous trip through the heart of Africa to rescue the missionary-explorer Dr. Livingstone. The British were both discovering and conquering India, and adventurers returned to the South Seas to find Captain Cook's paradise. But we must remember that the camera was not yet in general use. Only artists could bring the flavor of such places to the fascinated public in

Kindred Spirits, by Asher B.
Durand, 1849 *Collection of the
New York Public Library. Astor,
Lenox and Tilden Foundations*

Coast Scene with Figures, by John Frederick Kensett, 1869 *Wadsworth Atheneum, Hartford, Conn.*
Ella Gallup Sumner and Mary Catlin Sumner Collection

The Voyage of Life: Childhood, by Thomas Cole, 1842 National Gallery of Art,
Washington, D.C. Ailsa Mellon Bruce Fund

The Voyage of Life: Youth, by Thomas Cole, 1842 National Gallery of Art,
Washington, D.C. Ailsa Mellon Bruce Fund

The Voyage of Life: Manhood, by Thomas Cole, 1842 National Gallery of Art,
Washington, D.C. Ailsa Mellon Bruce Fund

The Voyage of Life: Old Age, by Thomas Cole, 1842 National Gallery of Art,
Washington, D.C. Ailsa Mellon Bruce Fund

Autumn—on the Hudson River, by Jasper Francis Cropsey, 1860   National Gallery of Art, Washington, D.C.
Gift of the Avalon Foundation

Morning in the Tropics, by Frederic E. Church, 1877   *National Gallery of Art, Washington, D.C. Gift of the Avalon Foundation*

Europe and the United States. Church visited the Holy Land, the Alps, and the isles of Greece; but what interested him most were the unvisited regions of the Western Hemisphere. The explorations of Baron Humbolt, the German naturalist, inspired him. His friend, Cyrus W. Field (who later financed the laying of the Atlantic cable) was determined to find his brother, who had disappeared in South America. Church joined him on his desperate search, and saw Ecuador and Colombia. Everywhere Church went, he painted—everything from the floating icebergs of Labrador to the hidden valleys and volcanoes of the Andes. In his *Morning in the Tropics* we see the thick, tangled foliage of the jungle under the steamy pall of a foggy, brooding tropical morning. God, as Church saw it, was everywhere; and we may notice that

the light of the sun, reflected on the water, forms a cross. Thousands of New Yorkers filed in to see one of Church's largest paintings, *The Heart of the Andes,* shown in a darkened room decorated with Ecuadorian palms and illuminated by gaslights. It was the sensation of the year 1859.

When rheumatism made it impossible for Church to paint with his right hand, he painted with his left; and when he could paint no longer, he went on with his travels, an explorer and scientist at heart. He was one of the first Americans to appreciate the pre-Columbian art of the South American Indians, and he collected it in his home on the Hudson. What an extraordinary home it was, a Moorish palace in the Catskills, full of a strange combination of South American objects and Romantic paintings.

Church's Moorish Palace might strike us as unusual in a world of Greek Revival temples, but the Romantics did not care for the neat lines of Classical architecture. They preferred the more mysterious forms of other periods. P. T. Barnum, the circus impressario, lived in a fantasy that resembled an Iranian mosque. But Gothic architecture with its pointed arches and spidery spires, which suggested so many Romantic tales of the Middle Ages, was by far the favorite. And so, with Romanticism came the Gothic Revival. As America grew swiftly, villages became cities—in the Middle West, and along the banks of the Mississippi. Throughout the country a world of "Gothic" public buildings, schools, libraries, and churches grew up alongside those of the Greek Revival. In private homes ceilings became higher, windows narrower. Turrets and towers were added, and the fantastical delights of jigsawed "gingerbread" decoration.

Of America's Romantic artists, two remain to hold our imagination—two who lived cut off from the world, creating visions from their imagination that haunt us a hundred and more years later.

St. Patrick's Cathedral, New York, designed by James Renwick, 1858–79 *Museum of the City of New York*

William Rimmer (1816–1879) was perhaps America's greatest Romantic sculptor. Rimmer came to Boston from Nova Scotia when he was ten. There he lived in poverty with a father who was half mad, and who thought he was the son of the King of France. Young Rimmer was brought up on wild tales and prepared for an imaginary future as a figure of royalty. In fact, he remained in poverty all his life, although he studied everything from typesetting to medicine and was a highly respected lecturer on anatomy to both artists and physicians. His figure of the *Falling Gladiator* (page 86) seems to tell us of the torture of someone who has labored and suffered defeat. If we compare it with Morse's *Dying Hercules* (page 76), we can see that, although on the surface they are very much alike, Morse's is a showpiece while Rimmer's springs from life's agonies.

Perhaps strangest of all was Albert Pinkham Ryder (1847–1917), a great (some think the greatest) landscapist of the nineteenth century. Unlike Cole, Ryder did not wander the countryside with his canvases under his arm. He lived for half a century in a tiny New York apartment, and rarely left it.

Ryder was the son of a seafaring family of New Bedford, Massachusetts, then the whaling capital of the world. At twenty he came to New York and settled in an apartment on West Fifteenth Street, which was soon enough filled with a clutter of possessions. The fact that he did not wander far made little difference to his work; his paintings, like Allston's, were "the product of a mind that lived in a world of its own." In his crowded quarters he painted pictures of village life or the sea, or scenes from the Bible, Shakespeare, the opera, or the poetry of the Romantics—Byron, Coleridge, Poe, and others. The leaves on the trees in his city garden might, to his inner eye, appear the forest of Arden from Shakespeare's *As You Like It*. Ryder would nightly walk the city streets in an old coat and stocking cap, his eyes turned to the windy clouds or brilliant skies which would later fill his paintings. He knew the sea firsthand, having sailed several times to Europe, not to see its great works of art, but to observe the ocean itself on the way.

Falling Gladiator, by William Rimmer, c. 1860
The Metropolitan Museum of Art. Rimmer Memorial Society Committee and Rogers Fund, 1907

But Ryder did not observe nature as Cole did, to capture the appearance of leaves, the effect of light, the impression of a view. He felt that "the eyes must see nought but the image beyond," and that "art does not render visible, but makes visible." His *Siegfried and the Rhine Maidens* was painted in forty-eight hours of fevered work after seeing a performance of Wagner's opera. We do not see carefully detailed trees or human figures; rather, a few large shapes are built up in thick paint that bring the scene to our eyes. Yet these shadowy forms, which we can only make out by studying the canvas closely, tell us far more than a neatly detailed picture could. We can almost hear the thunder of Wagner's music. The movement of the enchanted maidens' arms is repeated and magnified by the branches of the trees, and there is even more drama in the sky

than on the earth. Ryder wrote, "What avails a storm cloud accurate in color if the storm is not within." The storm is there, and the moon illuminates the scene like lightning. Ryder's canvases, like Allston's, are memories of a dream, but not the artist's dream alone. When we look at them, we feel a twinge of memory. Something tells us we have dreamed these dreams ourselves.

Ryder experimented with the use of thick layers of paint. Unfortunately, over the years his canvases have cracked and aged, but this has not weakened their hold on our imagination. Like Allston, Cole, and so many of the Romantics, Ryder was also a poet. He wrote:

> Who knows what God knows?
> His hand he never shows,
> Yet miracles with less are wrought
> Even with a thought.

The Realists

Not all Americans of the nineteenth century wanted to escape into a dream world of perfect beauty or dramatic excitement. Some were pleased and fascinated or amused by the real world around them. They read with a chuckle the books of Mark Twain and the lively stories of William Dean Howells. If they lived in the fast-growing city, they would sing the songs of Stephen Foster and try to remember every detail of childhoods spent in the country villages of the North, or the plantations of the South. As real problems arose, the problems of the terrible division of the people that led to the Civil War, Americans turned more of their attention to their country, and the life they led. They loved American life as it was lived, and they wanted to read about it in their books and see it in their art. As we have seen, realism has always been important in American art.

What are called "genre" paintings—scenes of everyday life—now became popular. William Sidney Mount (1807–1868), one of the first and most successful painters of such pictures, lived exactly the life we might imagine from his paintings. He was born in Stony Brook, Long Island, the nephew of a greengrocer who wrote comic

Siegfried and the Rhine Maidens, by Albert Pinkham Ryder, c. 1888–91   *National Gallery of Art, Washington, D.C. Andrew W. Mellon Collection*

operas and serenaded his customers on the piano. Mount could have gone to Europe to study art, but he didn't wish to. He found life so enjoyable on Long Island that he was positively grateful that Adam and Eve had left Eden. He would trundle down country lanes in his own horse-drawn studio, to paint "the happy but unstudied circumstance the moment should offer" of ladies gossiping, or children misbehaving. When he was not painting, Mount liked to play at country dances on an instrument of his own inventing called the "Yankee Fiddle or Cradle of Harmony." He was a great believer in the pleasures of life, and he saw only life's sunny side. He never painted men working, but only farmers resting and enjoying themselves, as in his *Farmers Nooning*.

The finest of the "genre" painters was certainly George Caleb Bingham (1811–1879). Bingham grew up in the frontier town of Franklin, Missouri, a shoeless farm boy whose widowed mother had known better days. Like most frontier boys, young Bingham learned a bit of everything: some cabinetmaking, some cigar rolling, some theology and law, and how to copy engravings. It was when the painter Chester Harding passed through Franklin on his way to find and paint Daniel Boone that Bingham decided he wanted a future as an artist.

Along the Missouri, as along the Mississippi and the other rivers of the Middle West, stood towns that were separated by deep forest. It was the river that united them, and many of the settlers lived as much on the river as on land. The Mississippi itself was muddy and swarmed with flies. But up and down it sailed everything from flatboats carrying pork, flour, whisky, tobacco, cattle, and horses, to floating palaces with mirrors, mahogany fittings, and ten-course dinners. We all know how the life of the river fascinated Samuel Clemens. So much, in fact, that he

Farmers Nooning, by William Sidney Mount, 1836   *Courtesy, Melville Collection, Suffolk Museum and Carriage House, Stony Brook, Long Island*

Raftsmen Playing Cards, by George Caleb Bingham, 1847   *The St. Louis Art Museum*

took as his pen name the riverboat pilot's call, "Mark Twain." He set out to "learn the river" and to become "personally and familiarly acquainted with all the different types of human nature that are to be found in fiction, biography or history." Bingham, too, had "learned the river." In his *Raftsmen Playing Cards* we see exactly the kind of raft in which Huck Finn took off on his Mississippi adventure. But these are the men of the river. And each character is a very "different type of human nature." As one critic wrote when the painting was first presented: "One of the players, rather a young man, . . . a 'hard case,' has just thrown down a card and is awaiting a result; while his antagonist, a somewhat older person . . . is hesitating and troubled at the appearance of the game. The young man looking over his shoulder appears a mean and cunning scamp, probably the black sheep of a good family, a sort of vagabond idler. The other person who is watching the progress of the players is a middle aged man, industrious, frugal, and might be the respectable proprietor of the raft."

The subjects that Bingham painted were realistic. The way he painted them was not. His pictures were not created in the open air, but carefully composed in his studio. His raftsmen appear in lights and shadows that are almost too sharply clear. Behind them the river is enveloped in a hazy, almost "Romantic" mist. The figures are as posed as statuary. Bingham has taken the "grand style" we might expect of Benjamin West, and used it to portray scenes of the everyday life of the frontier, giving to them strength and power.

89

Hound and Hunter, by Winslow Homer, 1892   National Gallery of Art, Washington, D.C. Gift of Stephen C. Clark

Breezing Up, by Winslow Homer, 1876   National Gallery of Art, Washington, D.C. Gift of the W. L. and May T. Mellon Foundation

The paintings of Bingham and the other "genre" artists have great charm, but they are not great art. Two of the Realists *were* among America's greatest painters. Winslow Homer (1836–1910) and Thomas Eakins (1844–1916) were artists whose pictures did not tell charming or interesting stories; they portrayed nature and struggles of everyday life as they knew them to be.

Winslow Homer was the son of a hardware importer, one of a long line of New Englanders. Like Bingham, he spent his childhood out-of-doors. At the age of nineteen, he first studied lithography. This was a time when more and more newspapers and magazines were springing up throughout the country, and these publications were illustrated by woodcuts of artists' sketches of daily events. It was as woodcut illustrator that Homer began his career. He drew everything from pretty girls for the covers of sheet music to comic pictures of seaside bathers. And he was largely self-taught. In his later years he said, "If a man wants to be an artist, he should never look at pictures."

During the Civil War, *Harper's Weekly* sent young Homer to sketch at the front. Now his art took a more serious turn. He sent back drawings that depicted the war as it was actually fought; here were no adorable little drummer boys and billowing flags, but bedraggled and torn soldiers, hardly able to go on. Homer did more than sketch; he taught himself to paint, not in the delicate washes of color that Bingham so often used, but in thick paint direct from the palette. The result was *Prisoners from the Front*, which showed the war as Americans, Northerners and Southerners alike, knew it to be. Here is reality as it had never been painted in America. Three Confederate prisoners stand before a Union officer. The officer is calm. The rumpled captives appear exhausted and confused, and only one shows a spark of life. Their gestures are not grandiose or dramatic—the figures might have been caught in a snapshot, simply standing. They are not surrounded by a "Romantic" haze, but stand in the true light of day. The muddy grass

Prisoners from the Front, by Winslow Homer, 1866 *The Metropolitan Museum of Art. Gift of Mrs. Frank* B. Porter, *1922*

Snap the Whip, by Winslow Homer, 1872   *The Butler Institute of American Art, Youngstown, Ohio*

at their feet is not pretty. If we compare this picture with West's *The Death of Wolfe* (page 56), considered a great work of "realism" in its time, we can tell how true to reality Homer's paintings actually are.

After the war, Homer wanted to return to nature. He wandered through New England as far as the White Mountains, down the Jersey shore, and south to Virginia. Everywhere he painted exactly what met his eye: farm and country life, the life of blacks in the South, woodsmen and fishermen. He painted vacationers under their parasols, a classroom, a croquet match. He often painted children at play, as in *Snap the Whip*. These might be Tom Sawyer and his barefoot friends, with their trousers rolled up and their caps pulled over their eyes. Homer painted not what was pretty, but what was real. Yet his paintings were not without drama or excitement. In fact, he liked to paint scenes of manly adventure. In *Hound and Hunter* (page 90), we see a boy in his boat struggling with a deer in the icy waters of a stream.

In later life, Homer was drawn to the sea. He visited the fishing villages of England, and finally settled at Prout's Neck on the rocky Maine coast. One subject interested him: humanity's struggle with nature, and above all, with the sea. No American artist has ever been able to paint the sea, the brilliant or shadowed sunlight, or the billowing wind as Homer did. In *Breezing Up* (page 91), we see again Homer's shoeless boys. We can almost feel the tension on the ropes that hold the sail. In paintings like this, we can tell what direction the wind is coming from and how hard it is blowing; we know that the weak sun will soon disappear, and that trouble brews in the darkening sea.

Homer was described as "a quiet little man." He kept to himself, and saw few people other than the fishermen whose lives he painted. But he did travel. He accompanied the fishing fleet to the Grand Banks off Newfoundland; and in the winters he visited Florida, Cuba, and the Bahamas, always keeping to the coast. In *The Gulf Stream*, we see a Bahamian fishing boat in trouble.

Its mast is broken, and the water is alive with sharks. But the fisherman, dazed and exhausted, faces his fate with courage. There are no dramatic gestures. Well over a century has passed since Copley painted *Watson and the Shark*.

In his youth Homer painted men and women at work and play, in middle age he painted man's struggle with nature, but toward the end of his life human figures disappeared from his pictures. He painted nature itself—the endless beating of the seas upon the rocky coast.

Thomas Eakins was a Philadelphia boy who decided to be an artist early in life. He studied, naturally enough, at the Pennsylvania Academy. Eakins, like Charles Willson Peale, loved realism with the love of a scientist; again like Peale, if he had not been an artist, he would have devoted his life to science or mathematics.

In his early twenties Eakins went to Paris, where he mastered the craft of painting pure and simple. But the art of France did not interest him. He was excited by the realism he saw in the work of certain Spanish painters, such as Diego Velásquez, the great painter of the seventeenth-century Spanish court. He wrote home excitedly. In such pictures, he said, "You can see what o'clock it is, whether morning or afternoon, if it is hot or cold, winter or summer, and which kind of people are there and what they are doing." But despite his experiences, his roots clung to the reality of America, and he never felt a trip to Europe was important for American artists. He later told his students that their "first desire should be to remain in America, to peer deeper into the heart of American life." Eakins returned home as soon as possible, and spent the rest of his life in Philadelphia.

Like Winslow Homer, whose art he admired, Eakins loved the outdoor life. He painted sportsmen boating, fishing, swimming, and hunting. He himself was an oarsman, and a friend of the Biglin brothers, sculling champions whom he painted. Here we see Eakins' scientific realism at work. He observed his subjects carefully, but this was not enough. To begin with, the anatomy of the figures must be perfect. Eakins studied anatomy, not merely from the plaster casts at the Pennsylvania Academy, but by observing dissections at a medical college. Moreover, he made use

The Gulf Stream, by Winslow Homer, 1899   *The Metropolitan Museum of Art. Wolfe Fund, 1906*

The Biglin Brothers Racing, by Thomas Eakins, c. 1873   National Gallery of Art, Washington, D.C.
Gift of Mr. and Mrs. Cornelius Vanderbilt Whitney

of the camera to see exactly how the human body looked when caught in motion. (It is interesting that when the first photographs appeared, they were not expected to replace art; they were used by artists who wanted to study more closely the reality they wished to paint.) Next, Eakins studied the light he wanted to portray. Often he would pose rag models on the roof of his studio in order to capture the light exactly. Finally, the composition and perspective must be perfect. For this Eakins would create complicated mechanical drawings like the one for *John Biglin in a Single Scull.* He placed his figures perfectly in space. The result of all this careful study was a reality that seemed casual and unposed.

We have seen that the painting of tellingly real portraits has a long history in America, from the portrait of the aged Anne Pollard to the paintings of Copley and beyond. Many Americans may have wanted to be flattered by their portraits—and some were—yet time and again reality crept in.

But of all the painters of the true faces of America, the greatest was Thomas Eakins. Let us look at some of these faces. We yearn to know more about every one of them: the singer of *The Pathetic Song,* a woman seized by such sadness we think the life must have been wrung out of her, despite her elegant and expensive dress; or *Mrs. Edith Mahon,* whose eyes are so filled with experience we want to pour out our hearts to her. These are members of Eakins' circle of friends—scientists, teachers, wealthy widows, and such. No wonder Walt Whitman, another close friend, said of Eakins, "I never knew of but one artist, and that's Tom Eakins, who could resist the temptation to see what they thought ought to be, rather than what is." No wonder, as he said, "Tom's portraits . . . are not a remaking of life, but life . . . just as it is, as they are." But the truth did not always please. Some of Eakins' friends were outraged by the way the artist saw them. Others paid for their portraits, and then quietly burned them.

Perspective Drawing for John Biglin in a Single Scull, by Thomas Eakins, 1873–74   *Courtesy, Museum of Fine Arts, Boston. Gift of Cornelius V. Whitney*

The Pathetic Song, by Thomas Eakins, 1881 *In the collection of the Corcoran Gallery of Art*

Mrs. Edith Mahon, by Thomas Eakins, 1904 *Smith College Museum of Art*

Many feel that Eakins' insistence on absolute realism destroyed his career. His great painting entitled *The Gross Clinic* was refused exhibition. It depicted the scene of an operation and was thought so bloody that it would frighten women and children. Eakins was made Director of the Pennsylvania Academy, but lost his position when he insisted that live nude male models replace the dusty plaster casts, even in classes with women students. Today, we see Eakins as one of America's greatest artists. Surely none was ever able to "peer deeper into the heart of American life."

The Artist Goes West

By 1830 the United States was settled as far as the banks of the Mississippi. Between these settlements and the Pacific Ocean lay the Great Plains, where the Plains Indians roamed at the height of their power—riding horseback, shooting buffalo with guns, and living more richly than ever before. Beyond lay the Rocky Mountains, so mysterious they were known only from the tales of a few travelers. Would the white settlers go farther? There were those, at the time, who thought they would not. But in 1849 gold was discovered in California, while from the East wave after wave of land-hungry settlers pushed to the Mississippi and beyond. All eyes were on the great, unknown barrier. People had heard tales, but what was there to see? A few artist-adventurers were tempted to venture into the wilderness, to record what was there before it was destroyed, and to hint to the Easterners what lay beyond the river.

It was neither the people nor the mountains of the American frontier that fascinated John Audubon (1785–1851), but its wildlife. Audubon was a mysterious, dashing figure throughout his life. He was born the son of a Haitian chambermaid and a French sea captain. His mother died young, and Audubon was taken to France by his father. Even as a boy his hobby was ornithology, and he spent the long hours of his childhood drawing pictures of birds. He returned to America at eighteen, a strange figure who went out to shoot birds in silken hose and knee breeches. After a series of misadventures, leading to debtors' prison, Audubon decided to try his hand at what he had always enjoyed—painting birds. He submitted some of his pictures to the Western Museum in Cincinnati, and they were greeted with praise. This warm encouragement, from an unknown critic in a frontier town, led Audubon to his life's work. He decided to paint *all* the species of birds extant at that time in America, and to depict them in their natural setting, just as he found them.

In the year 1820 he set out on a flatboat down the Mississippi. He took with him nothing but a gun, a drawing book, and paints. Like Thomas Cole, who at that moment was laboring to paint portraits for his supper in the Ohio Valley, he carried a flute. During the next six years Audubon traveled throughout the American frontier, going as far as Labrador. He made hundreds of paintings of the thousands of bird specimens he collected, each one caught in natural motion, its graceful body outlined sharply. Each painting was correct in every detail, and every bird was painted its exact size. Audubon's superb compositions are complete with the leaves of the trees in which the birds nested, the nests themselves, and the insects, berries, fruits, flowers, and snakes that were part of their "habitat," the natural world in which they lived out their lives.

Audubon's strange work met with great success. His huge folio, *The Birds of America,* published in the form of prints, was bought by a wide audience, including the King of England. Audubon had gone into the wilderness, discovered its secrets, and given them to the world.

But what of the people of the wilderness? How much did Easterners know of the lives of the Indians themselves? To writers and artists of the Romantic movement, Indians were "noble savages," people who lived simply, in harmony with nature. On the other hand, frontiersmen had had experiences that could only fill them with fear. Indian raids were still frequent. One of the bloodiest occurred in the Wyoming Valley of Pennsylvania shortly after the Revolution, when a group of Tories joined with the Indians to attack frontier settlements. Many settlers were taken prisoner by

Columbia Jay, by John James Audubon
(from *The Birds of America,* Plate 96) *National Gallery of Art, Washington, D.C. Gift of Mrs. Walter B. James*

Columbia Jay
GARRULUS COLUMBIANUS

the Indians and later freed. Among them was the mother of the man who would one day become the Indians' closest friend, George Catlin (1796–1872).

As a child, Catlin loved to "play Indian." His play was so realistic, in fact, that he carried for the rest of his life the scar of a toy tomahawk. His parents sent him to law school, but Catlin taught himself to paint. Unfortunately, he could never manage anatomy correctly, and his portraits of friends and neighbors were miserable failures. He happened, however, to be in Philadelphia one day in 1824 when a delegation of Far West Indians came to town "in all their classic beauty with shield and helmet, tunic and manteau—tinted and tasseled off exactly for the painters palette." Young Catlin was deeply impressed. He made some sketches and realized they were by far the best he had ever done. He had seen Peale's Natural History Museum, and this, too, inspired him. He decided he would found an "Indian Gallery" containing pictures, which he himself would paint, of members of all the Indian tribes that still existed in North America. Like Audubon, he felt he must record every detail of a world still in its "natural state," before it disappeared. Catlin felt the Indian was doomed, and that "the history and customs of such a people, preserved by pictorial illustrations, are themes worthy of the lifetime of one man, and nothing short of the loss of my life shall prevent me from visiting their country, and of becoming their historian."

Catlin was as good as his word. In 1830 he set out, intending to visit all the known North American Indian tribes and bring home portraits of their important leaders, views of their villages, pictures of their members playing and going about their daily tasks, and written notes on their "character and history." He went first to Saint Louis, then the muddy and fly-blown territorial capital, where he painted the Indian chieftains who often visited. From this point, he took off to crisscross the wilderness: up the Missouri on the first steamboat ever to sail its waters, as far as Fort Union in South Dakota; then to the present Tulsa and the plains of the Southwest; then up the Mississippi and Des Moines rivers. During his travels he fell ill among the Comanches, and found the sacred mineral of which peace pipes were made (now called "catlinite").

The Indians that Catlin met had seen few white people, and they greeted him with friendship. Everywhere he went, he sketched, drew, and painted. Catlin worked always at top speed, wanting to record everything as quickly as possible before moving on. Once, in 1832, he painted 135 pictures in 86 days, during which he traveled 1500 miles, all the while meeting Indians, getting to know them, and joining them in their hunts and games. It was not easy. Many Indians were superstitious and did not want their portraits painted. Some even feared that if they were painted with their eyes open, they would never sleep again. Often Catlin was not allowed to paint the women until the men had sat for their portraits. Once, when he painted the profile of a brave, a member of an enemy tribe claimed that the picture was proof that the sitter was only half a man. The result was bloodshed. Catlin painted not only portraits but landscapes, pictures of villages, and the habits and customs of the Indians and their ceremonies. He was, in fact, the first white artist to paint the buffalo.

With the Indians themselves, Catlin had a good and lasting friendship. He found them beings of "beauty and wildness," happier than "kings and emperors." To him they were "knights of the forest, whose lives are lives of chivalry." Above all, he wanted to make white people feel that the Indians had "thoughts, reasons, sympathies like our own." Even the torture rites of "coming-of-age" did not discourage him. He understood them as an Indian understood them, as a proof of courage. The results of Catlin's work were paintings of wild beauty, hundreds of them. If the anatomy of his figures is not perfect, it makes little difference. Catlin saw the beauty of Indian dress. In fact, he was one of the first Americans to understand the decorative art of the American Indians. He made it part of his own art, as we can see in his painting *Old Bear, Mandan Medicine Man*. This is more than a decorative design. We can tell that it is a painting of a man Catlin knew. And when Catlin painted ceremonies, like *Bull Dance, Part of*

Old Bear, Mandan Medicine Man, by George Catlin, 1832   *Courtesy of Smithsonian Institution*

Okipa Ceremony (page 102), we can feel the tension and excitement. We can almost hear the throbbing of the drums.

By the mid-1850s the Gold Rush had swept thousands of Americans clear across Catlin's West to the Pacific Coast. Men, women, and children had crossed the Rockies, enduring great hardship, and had discovered a new land. Stories of this dangerous, magnificent country circulated. But what did this new country look like? The answer was brought back by an artist of German birth, Albert Bierstadt (1830–1902).

Bierstadt, who was trained to paint in Ger-

many, accompanied a government surveying expedition to the Rocky Mountains, and there he found the proper subject for his brush. His *The Rocky Mountains* (page 103) caused as much excitement among the public as Church's paintings of the Andes had, shortly before. Here was the true sweep, the true grandeur of the West; it was as Easterners imagined, hoped it would be. Bierstadt liked to fill his paintings with figures, and here we see an entire Indian encampment. He was a "Romantic," and *The Rocky Mountains* has all the drama of a Romantic landscape: the peaks are higher, more snowy than reality; the gorges are

Bull Dance, Part of Okipa Ceremony, by George Catlin,   *Courtesy of Smithsonian Institution*

deeper. Dramatic lights and shadows are cast by unseen clouds above.

Bierstadt only sketched in the Rockies. His larger paintings were completed in his studio in New York. Unlike Church, he was not always careful to represent rocks and foliage as he actually found them. In fact, some critics felt his paintings looked like the Swiss Alps with buffalo and Indians. Still, such paintings stirred people in the East. Many a family set off with their children and their few possessions in a covered wagon, their livestock trailing behind and Bierstadt's images in their hearts.

If Catlin was the painter of the American Indian, and Bierstadt the portrayer of the Rocky Mountains, the artist of the Western cowboys and settlers was Frederic Remington (1861–1909).

Born in Canton, New York, the son of a wealthy publisher, Remington was a boxer and a football player at Yale—the last man one would expect to become the artist of the Old West. But as a boy he loved horses, and fed on the journals of George Catlin and Lewis and Clark. At the age of nineteen, he left college to look for adventure. He traveled from Montana to Texas, as a cowpuncher and prospector. Remington had always been interested in journalism. Now he began to write about, and to paint and sketch, what he saw. The "Winning of the West" fascinated the East. Magazines and newspapers were crammed with accounts of prospectors' adventures, and of battles with Indians, rustlers, and other outlaws—all the tales that were then news and have since become legends. There were also stories by Bret Harte,

Richard Harding Davis, Joaquin Miller, and many more. Often these were illustrated by sketches and paintings from Remington's hand, but it was as a sculptor that Remington was the greater artist.

Remington was fascinated by horses. He could tell the difference between the horses that the Indians rode in Arizona and those they rode in Montana. As a sculptor, he created small bronzes of human figures—Indians or cowboys on horseback, or fallen off. Few sculptors have been more at ease portraying horses in action. Often even Remington's sculptures tell stories of excitement or suspense. *The Old Dragoons* (page 104) actually represents a running fight between two soldiers and two Indian braves in all its stampeding fury.

American Naive Painting

During most of the nineteenth century, four out of every five Americans lived "on the land," on farms and in the small towns. In the middle of the

century, before a network of railways covered the country, the dweller of a village in central Connecticut might live two days' journey from Boston, and three days' from New York. Many never visited the large cities where most of the great works of American art were to be seen. Yet they, too, wanted portraits of their loved ones and paintings to decorate their homes. What artists filled this need?

There were many of them, and they painted much in the style of the earliest artists, the painters who made portraits of the first settlers and the successful merchants of eighteenth-century America. Like these artists, they had little or no formal training. Many had never been to the large cities, and like artists of a hundred years earlier, who had never been to Europe, they often did not know what "great" works of art looked like unless they had seen a traveling painting like Rembrandt Peale's *Court of Death*. Like the painter of *Mrs. Freake and Baby Mary*, these artists had not learned about shading and modeling, so their

The Rocky Mountains, by Albert Bierstadt, 1863   *The Metropolitan Museum of Art, Rogers Fund, 1907*

The Old Dragoons, by Frederic Remington, 1905   *The Metropolitan Museum of Art, Rogers Fund, 1907*

pictures appear flat. They had little knowledge of human anatomy, and often the laws of perspective were a mystery to them. For this reason, they are called "Naive" painters. The word *naive,* according to the dictionary, means "showing natural simplicity . . . a lack of experience or information." Many of the Naive artists' lives are completely unknown to us. Often, we do not even known the artists' name. Still, if we look at their paintings, not for realism but for other qualities, we will find many that are fascinating, decorative, lively, fresh, free, and (that too-often-used word) beautiful.

Who were the Naive painters? Many were professional "itinerant" artists who traveled from village to village. Most were men, but some were women. As we have seen, Thomas Cole was such an artist. These traveling painters asked for room and board, and little else. A portrait of a child might go for as little as twenty cents, and flat likenesses were less expensive than those in which the artist tried a little modeling. The more successful traveled with ready-prepared canvases and colors: water, oil, and pastel. It is even possible that a few went so far as to spend the winter painting

faceless figures in splendid dress—men in handsome jackets and women with stiff lace collars. In summer they would take these canvases from town to town, filling in the faces. Whether this is true or not, many settlers never in their lives owned clothing as fine as appeared in their portraits.

Other artists were not so well off. They worked far from the cities and made their own colors from Indian pigments, just as West had done as a child. They would paint their pictures on anything that came to hand: pieces of wood, tin or zinc, window shades, table linoleum, bed ticking, fabrics, cardboard, or paper. At times, small pieces of paper or fabric would be glued or stitched together to make a surface on which to paint. They could also lend their talents to painting signs, carriages, or even houses. When called upon, their paintings replaced wallpaper, which was rare and expensive.

But the Naive artists were not all itinerant painters. Many were "Sunday artists," farmers, housewives, shopkeepers and such—who were talented and painted in their spare time. We must remember that these were the days when Americans across the country did everything for themselves: sewing, weaving, dyeing, making furniture, or making candles and soap—all were done at home. If a man could build his own house, why could he not paint the pictures that hung on its walls?

Portraits were all-important. The painting of *Mrs. Mayer and Daughter* by Ammi Phillips (1788–1865) appears very flat. The figures are almost without shadow. But what a masterpiece of graceful line and startling color this is, and with what delicacy and beauty the transparent lace of the bonnet and collar is painted! The artist may have had difficulty with the anatomy of the hands, but the problem was solved by making them gracefully balanced shapes. Above all, this is a brilliant likeness. We think we know exactly what Mrs. Mayer looked like, and how her child resembled her. Of Ammi Phillips we know only that he was a successful itinerant painter for fifty years, working in Connecticut, Massachusetts, and New York.

Often the Naive portraits are more imagina-

Mrs. Mayer and Daughter, attributed to Ammi Phillips, c. 1835   *The Metropolitan Museum of Art.*
Gift of Edgar William and Bernice Chrysler Garbisch, 1962

Emma Van Name, by an unknown artist, c. 1795   *Oil on canvas. 29 × 23 inches. Collection of Whitney Museum of American Art. Gift of Edgar William and Bernice Chrysler Garbisch.*

tive than the works of serious portraitists of the cities. The picture of *Emma Van Name*, shown here, must have been painted in June. It is really more of a painting of the greed for strawberries than of a little girl. There is something familiar about this painting. It has the dark background and square tiled floor of *Alice Mason* (page 35), painted more than a hundred years earlier. In the rural parts of the country, artistic styles were not quickly forgotten. There is also something strange about the picture. The goblet of strawberries is half as high as the child herself. In fact, Emma may have been very tiny, and much younger than she seems.

The Naive artists did not paint portraits alone. They also painted landscapes, often scenes with many people. Sometimes these were historical events, like *Custer's Last Fight* by W. J. Wallack. This picture was painted in Nebraska shortly after the famous battle of Little Big Horn, where the stubborn cavalry leader George Armstrong Custer led a charge against the Sioux Indians and was slaughtered.

The paintings of the Naive artists tell us more about daily life in America in the nineteenth century than any book. This is so because the Naive artists made a great point of painting every detail of life exactly as it was. Look, for example,

Custer's Last Fight, June 25, 1876, by W. J. Wallack, 1876   *Buffalo Bill Historical Center, Cody, Wyoming*

Flax Scutching Bee, by Linton Park, c. 1860   *National Gallery of Art, Washington, D.C. Gift of Edgar William and Bernice Chrysler Garbisch.*

at a *Flax Scutching Bee*. Flax scutching, the breaking down of flax fibers, is a difficult job, and the neighbors in a frontier community got together to help one another and make a party of it. Here the flax, on upright boards at the right, is being treated with a kind of paddle. Moreover, the neighbors seem to be having a good time doing it. Some are talking, some dancing and singing, and a few have had too much to drink. The artist, Linton Park (1826–1906), was by profession a lumberjack, and his picture tells more than merely how flax was prepared. It tells us about the bonnets and dresses, suits and hats, worn in a Pennsylvania frontier town. It tells us about log cabins, outhouses, fences, barns, and the cutting of trees and preparing of timber—all those details of life which might otherwise have been forgotten.

Some of the most delightful of all Naive paintings are the work of Edward Hicks (1780–1849), who lived in Bucks County, Pennsylvania, and painted for the sheer pleasure of painting. He was by trade a coach and sign painter, and also a famous Quaker preacher. One of his favorite subjects, which he painted over and over again, was the *Peaceable Kingdom,* the biblical Kingdom of God, where the lion would lie down with the lamb. To Hicks, the forests and fields of his native Pennsylvania were to be the Peaceable Kingdom; and the scene of William Penn signing his treaty with the Indians is sometimes included in the background. Here we see not only the lion lying down with the lamb, but a bear nuzzling a cow and a wolf snuggling up to a ewe and a goat. In these paintings the children who play peacefully with the wild animals are Hicks' own, and the lion is the artist himself. As Hicks grew older, so did the lions in his Peaceable Kingdoms.

The painting *A City of Fantasy* (page 110), by an unknown artist, may be strangest of all. In the foreground we see a city at the meeting of two rivers, combining in a whimsical way the architecture of many periods, buildings the artist must have seen in prints and engravings of the cities of Europe. The sailing ships in the bay are of the date of the painting itself. But in the background, in a cloudy mist that suggests a dream, we see a most extraordinary prophecy in paint. Here are towers that look, for all the world, exactly like modern

Peaceable Kingdom, by Edward Hicks, c. 1830   *Collection of Edgar William and Bernice Chrysler Garbisch*

A City of Fantasy, by an unknown artist, c. 1850 *National Gallery of Art, Washington, D.C. Gift of Edgar William and Bernice Chrysler Garbisch.*

skyscrapers. How could the artist, living in a small town in Massachusetts around 1850, have had such a vision? We do not know, and cannot even guess. But he must have had some sense of the tremendous growth that would take place in his country, and some idea of the oncoming age of science.

Impressionism

The end of the nineteenth century was an era of experimentation throughout the Western world. As we have seen, in the small towns and on the frontier, life was much as it had been a century before. But in the cities, it was a time of great progress. The steam engine, the sewing machine, and the reaper were in the past. Americans now experimented with the harvester, the typewriter, electric light, and the telephone. Everywhere, people were examining the world around them in a new, more scientific way.

In France, a group of artists felt displeased with the usual manner of painting as it was taught. They were of the opinion that artists were instructed to paint what the mind knew should be in the picture, but not what they felt the eye actually saw. When artists paint gardens, they argued, they are apt to paint every flower, every leaf and stem, all neatly outlined. But when we look at a garden, what do we actually see? We see bright splashes of color, and our mind fills in the rest. When an artist paints a horse running, the four legs of the horse are painted because the artist knows they are there.

The Boating Party, by Mary Cassatt, 1893–94
*National Gallery of Art, Washington, D.C.
Chester Dale Collection*

But when we look at a running horse, do we see all four legs so clearly?

This group of painters wanted to capture on their canvases only what they actually saw. It had been discovered that the eye in fact sees tiny patches of color which blend together to form larger shapes. These artists used strokes of brilliant, pure colors to create the fleeting effect that any scene makes on the eye. Only when seen at a certain distance do these splashes of color melt into one another, and forms appear. One such canvas was jeeringly called an "impression" by a critic, and the name stuck. These painters were called "Impressionists." Among them were many artists now famous—Edouard Manet, Claude Monet, Pierre Auguste Renoir, Edgar Degas. In this group of experimental French painters, there was also an American woman, Mary Cassatt (1845–1926).

Mary Cassatt was a strong-minded woman from Alleghany City, Pennsylvania, the daughter of a wealthy broker. She had studied painting at the Pennsylvania Academy at the same time that Eakins was a student there. In her early twenties she had departed for Paris to devote her life to art, despite her father's disapproval. But approval was of no great importance to Mary Cassatt. She was soon experimenting with the most disapproved of all styles of painting, Impressionism. She became a close friend of Edgar Degas, a strange, lonely man who is known for his Impressionist paintings of Parisian life: the theaters, ballet, or the horse races. It was he who invited her to join the Impressionists and to exhibit her work with theirs. Cassatt's style was very like Degas' own. With the loose, free brush strokes of the Impressionists, she suggested figures more full of life than most painters who carefully and neatly set down the details of the sitter's appearance.

Cassatt rarely painted men. She was more interested in painting women, especially women with children. Although she never married, and had no children of her own, children delighted her; she painted them with an energy and charm rarely seen. Her children are not mere pretty, lifeless creatures, as children so often appear in paintings. With a few strokes of the brush, Cassatt creates live children with characters as marked as any adult's. The little boy who squirms to escape his mother's arms in *The Boating Party* (page 111) is not a pretty child in the usual sense. We can tell he is uncomfortable, and his intelligent face is puckered up under the shadow of his sun hat. In another minute he is going to cry, although his mother pays no attention. The dark figure of the rower pulling in one direction as the sail pulls in the other creates a strong, free composition. Neither the entire boat nor the whole sail appear. They are cut off, as they might be in a snapshot. Photography interested the Impressionists, especially Degas and Cassatt, and their compositions often seem to be rectangles cut from reality, like figures and objects seen in the frame of a photograph.

It was an American, James Abbott McNeill Whistler (1834–1903), who, more than perhaps anyone, brought Impressionism to the notice of the English-speaking world. But perhaps Whistler should not be called an American at all. Much of his childhood was spent abroad. At twenty-one he returned to Europe, and, like West, he never saw America again. Whistler went to Paris to study art seriously. He felt immediately drawn to the idea of the Impressionists.

Although his art was not entirely like that of most of the Impressionists, Whistler also broke down his vision into tiny dabs of color, from which he built up his forms, such as *The White Girl*. But what was most important to Whistler was the careful balance of shapes, of areas of color in his compositions. Above all, they must create a harmony, like the harmony of music. He wrote: "As music is the poetry of sound, so painting is the poetry of sight, and the subject has nothing to do with the harmony of sound and color." Whistler felt subject matter was so unimportant that the famous portrait of his mother was originally called simply *Arrangement in Black and Gray, Number 1*. His *White Girl*, a strange figure of a girl who might be a bride, was, for Whistler, a harmonious arrangement of white shapes of varying shades. He later called it *Symphony in White Number 1*. When it was exhibited in 1863, it won for Whistler immediate success.

The White Girl (Symphony in White, No. 1), by James McNeill Whistler, 1862 *National Gallery of Art, Washington, D.C. Harris Whittemore Collection*

In 1859 Whistler moved to London. We must try to imagine what Whistler the man was like. He was famous for his wit, and his sharp tongue. He was also a dandy, with hair carefully curled and mustache neatly waxed, who never was seen without a stick and yellow gloves. Above all, he was one of the most ill-humored men in Europe. He even went so far as to write a book entitled *The Gentle Art of Making Enemies*. There was only one man in England who was grouchier, and that was the critic John Ruskin. When Whistler exhibited a painting entitled

Mrs. Isaac Newton Phelps Stokes, by John Singer Sargent, 1887 *The Metropolitan Museum of Art. Bequest of Edith Mintum Stokes, 1938*

Nocturne in Black and Gold: The Falling Rocket, the two men came face to face. The canvas was an Impressionist painting of fireworks at night, suggested by dabs of brilliant color against darkness. Ruskin, who hated Impressionism, was outraged. He wrote, "I never expected to hear a coxcomb ask two hundred guineas for flinging a pot of paint in the public's face." Whistler sued. Impressionism itself was on trial, and the case was bitterly fought. Whistler (and Impressionism) won, but he was awarded only one farthing for his trouble.

Whistler practiced as a successful portraitist, but his strange symphonies of color were never as popular as the portraits of a younger fellow American who also lived most of his life in Europe, John Singer Sargent (1856–1925). Sargent was born in Florence, the son of a wealthy American family that had settled in Italy, and he studied in both Florence and Paris.

Sargent was known for his brilliant brushwork. Like Stuart before him, he could capture a likeness with a few strokes of the brush. When Mrs. Isaac Newton Phelps Stokes came into Sargent's studio from the tennis court, he decided to paint her exactly as he saw her. The result was a portrait of a lively young woman still out of breath from her game. Such was Sargent's talent that he might have been as great a portraitist as Eakins. But Sargent's success was based on the fact that, when necessary, he flattered his sitters, especially women. Among the wealthy in America, a portrait by Sargent was considered a sure sign of social position.

If character appeared in a person's face, it might appear in the painting; but Sargent did not look for it. He said, "I do not dig beneath the surface of things that do not appear before my eyes." In this way, he was like the Impressionists, who painted exactly what they saw, and no more. Form and color to them were all. In fact, when he was bored with portraits, as he often was, Sargent would paint quick, impressionistic sketches of life around him. Many of these seem to us far greater than the portraits for which he was famous. Sargent spent much time in Venice, and in his *Street in*

Street in Venice, by John Singer Sargent, 1882 *National Gallery of Art, Washington, D.C. Gift of the Avalon Foundation*

Allies Day, May 1917, by Childe Hassam   *National Gallery of Art, Washington, D.C. Gift of Ethelyn McKinney
in memory of her brother, Glenn Ford McKinney*

Admiral David Glasgow Farragut, by Augustus Saint-Gaudens, 1910   *The Metropolitan Museum of Art. Gift by subscription through the Saint-Gaudens Replica Committee, 1912*

Venice we can see how, with just a few of his brilliant brush strokes, he has captured the feeling of the dank Venetian street and its people.

Mary Cassatt's *The Mandolin Player* was the first Impressionist painting ever to be shown in America. A few years later, in 1886, an exhibition of over three hundred Impressionist paintings appeared in New York. Although it was greeted with the usual furor, Americans, who always understood experimentation, were quick to appreciate the new style. Whistler, Cassatt, and Sargent spent most of their lives abroad, but soon Impressionist painters were at work in America.

Artists like Childe Hassam (1859–1933), and William Merritt Chase (1849–1916) brought back from Paris the Impressionist's blaze of sunshine and worked side by side with Realists like Homer and Eakins, Romantics like Church, and even the Naive artists, still painting in the style of the eighteenth century.

Impressionism found its way to sculpture as well. In the portrait bust of *Admiral David Glasgow Farragut* by Augustus Saint-Gaudens (1848–1907) the broken surface of the bronze creates a lively, Impressionistic play of light, and we feel that, like the Impressionists, the sculptor

117

A Friendly Call, by William Merritt Chase, 1895   National Gallery of Art, Washington, D.C. Gift of Chester Dale

has quickly caught the appearance of the moment. Saint-Gaudens, who was born in Dublin, the son of a poor French shoemaker, was brought to America as an infant. He studied in France and Italy, however, and lived to become America's leading sculptor at the end of the nineteenth century.

Although many young artists went to Europe to study, it was no longer absolutely necessary. For the new millionaires of the nineteenth century, owning a fine collection of "old masters" became a symbol of social position, and huge sums of money were spent bringing the masterpieces of European art to the United States. In the 1870s New York's Metropolitan Museum was founded, and during the period museums with permanent exhibitions sprang up all over the country.

Other important changes were taking place. Photography had existed since 1839. One of its chief inventors, a Frenchman, L. J. M. Daguerre,

was himself a painter; Samuel F. B. Morse became a photographer; and artists like Church and Eakins used photography to assist their work. Sooner or later it was sure to have a far-reaching effect on art, and by the end of the century it was clear what the first effect would be. We have seen how important portrait painting was throughout the history of American art. Eakins and Sargent, however, were the last of the great American "face" painters. By the end of the century, photographs had replaced painted portraits for all but the wealthy. The small-town "Naive" portrait painter disappeared entirely.

More important still, the Impressionists had broken all that was visible into patterns of color, and now artists saw the world around them in a new way. They were free to experiment and to try to express more than could merely be captured in a snapshot. So it was that the nineteenth century ended with perhaps the greatest revolution in the entire history of art.

6
THE TWENTIETH CENTURY

A Century of Change

Few people born in America during the early years of this century could have imagined the violent and fantastic changes that would take place in their lifetimes. Within an incredibly short period, people would no longer jounce along in horse-drawn carriages and trolleys, but soar in spacecraft to the distant moon. Terrible wars would be fought between nations and millions would be killed. On the other hand, science would make it possible for men and women to live longer than they could have expected to in earlier days. Invention would follow invention—the automobile, the airplane, movies, television, and countless other examples of scientific progress that are taken for granted today but would have been called "miracles" in the year 1900.

It would be difficult, almost impossible, for people living at the beginning of the century, when Sargent was the most-admired portraitist and Mary Cassatt's paintings were considered outlandish blotches of color, to imagine the course

that art would take. How could they dream that, one day, sculptures of objects they could not recognize would hang on wires from the ceiling and move lazily in the breeze, or that scrap from a junk heap might be welded together to make a work of art far more valuable than any Sargent portrait, and admired by millions. How could they foresee an artist who would walk over his huge canvases, dribbling, splashing, and throwing paint, or that art lovers might take pleasure in seeing a soapbox, blown up in size, but otherwise unchanged. How did this come about? It did not happen all at once. Let us look at each change as it occurred.

The Eight and George Bellows

The development of portrait photography had put many painters out of work. In the past, an artist who wanted to experiment might earn a living painting portraits part of the time, and spend the rest painting what pleased him. Now, when artists were more anxious to experiment than ever, portraiture no longer offered a living.

At the turn of the century, however, there was a sudden growth of popular illustrated newspapers and magazines. These gave work to artists. And while camera portraits were much in demand, news photography had yet to develop. Artists were constantly needed to report current events, just as news photographers or television cameramen are today. Given an assignment, an artist would rush off to sketch either a disaster such as a fire or explosion, or the scene of a crime, a boxing match, a street accident, a costume party, a city celebration, or a political rally. The job could be a dangerous one. An illustrator might be sent into the middle of a Cuban battlefield to draw Theodore Roosevelt and his Rough Riders or to report riots in a city street.

To capture a feeling of energetic life and activity, these artists developed a style of rapid sketching that could be called a form of "expressionism." Expressionism is a word that will reappear frequently in the history of twentieth-century art. A picture is said to be "expressionistic" when the artist has deliberately exaggerated either the lines, shapes, or colors (or all three) to give his work a stronger feeling of movement or mood. In other words, an "expressionistic" artist makes us look at his picture and recognize the same strong feelings that he felt when he painted or drew his work.

At the turn of the century, a small group of Philadelphia artists who had earned their living as illustrators found themselves with too little opportunity to paint what they wanted in the way they wanted to paint it. Moving to New York, their group grew in numbers. Eight of these artists, who admired and encouraged one another's experimental works, banded together in 1908 and organized an exhibition at the Macbeth Galleries in New York City. They called themselves simply "The Eight."

The Eight wanted to break away from the strict rules of art schools and academies. They proclaimed that art should be "alive" and that painting—like writing—should express the artist's feelings about life as he saw it. They had in common a love for the big city, and the big city was the new American reality. During the twentieth century, more and more Americans would crowd into cities until the majority were city dwellers, something no one could have imagined a century before. The Eight wanted to express the action, the heart of the city. They wanted to wander its streets in search of interesting subjects, to paint and draw them as they looked, unscrubbed and full of life. New York offered exactly the kind of subject they liked to bring to life on canvas: slums and clotheslines, grim laborers, snow-clogged streets, plodding horses, very old people, and ragged children racing down littered alleys. On the brighter side, New York offered circuses and Central Park, breathtaking bridges, gliding riverboats, the tense thrills of wrestling and boxing rings, and the brightly costumed dancers, singers, acrobats, and slapstick comedians of the vaudeville houses. Because of the grim subjects most of the young artists chose to paint, they were jeeringly called the "Ash Can School." One critic accused them of being not only "apostles of ugliness" but also "a revolutionary gang."

The Eight were deeply concerned about the social conditions of the time. They felt that too great a distance separated the splendid manner in which the rich lived and the way the poor were crushed together in evil-smelling slums. Their paintings inspired by these grubby sights have been frequently described historically as "social realism." As we have seen, "realism," painting life as it is, has always been important in American art. As we have also seen, artists who went too far, like Eakins, were little appreciated by the public. It would take some time to convince the public that social realism could be called "art."

The leader of The Eight was Robert Henri (1865–1929), a bold and talkative painter who believed in breaking rules. The colorful story of the group, an important story in the history of American art, begins with Henri and the circle of friends who first fell under his influence in Philadelphia. Henri, whose original name was Robert Henry Cozad, was born in Cincinnati,

Ohio. While still a small child, he moved with his family to Nebraska where his father, a professional gambler, founded a town and named it Cozad in honor of the family. There they lived an uneventful life until Robert reached the age of seventeen, when his father shot and killed a man in a gunfight. The family was forced to flee, eventually catching up with one another in Denver. Still on the move, they decided to change their name and settle in New Jersey. Robert, whose ancestors were French, dropped his last name and changed his middle one, Henry, to its French form, "Henri." Nevertheless, he insisted on pronouncing it "Hen-rye" to make it sound as American as possible. To Henri, wanting to be as American as possible would always mean wanting to be democratic, individual, and down to earth in both his life and his work.

As had so many American artists, Henri studied at the Pennsylvania Academy and in Europe before settling down in Philadelphia. He be-

gan his long career as a teacher at the Philadelphia School of Design for Women in 1892, and it is as a teacher that he is best known. Unlike most instructors in the academies, he tried to make his students paint in their own personal way rather than in his style. Henri told his friends and students to keep their eyes open, and that beauty could be found everywhere. Henri himself was equally pleased to paint loving portraits of his wife or of people discovered in the swarming working-class districts of the city. Henri's portrait of *Eva Green,* for example, shows us a street child bursting with life, courage, sweetness, and humor. Looking at her, we feel as if we are making a new friend instead of simply examining a picture composed of the rapid, sweeping brush strokes of an artist no longer living.

Henri became known for the warm, hearty gatherings in his studio on Tuesday nights, at first in Philadelphia and later in New York. He was the center of a group of young artists, most

Eva Green, by Robert Henri, 1907
The Roland P. Murdock Collection.
Wichita Art Museum

122

Backyards, Greenwich Village, by John Sloan, 1914   *Oil on canvas. 40 × 50 inches.*
Collection of Whitney Museum of American Art

scrimping to earn a living at illustrating, and hoping and praying for better days. Henri encouraged them to take themselves seriously as painters and to work hard at perfecting their skills. Among them were John Sloan (1871–1951), who designed puzzles and posters, and William Glackens (1870–1938), the group's adventurer, who had taken a cattleboat to Europe and reported the war in Cuba. *Backyards, Greenwich Village* shows Sloan in one of his happiest moods. Greenwich Village is a neighborhood of New York in which many artists still live, in the winding old streets where painters, poets, and writers of past generations had their homes and studios. But here we see a scene of family life, of children at play in the crowded backyards of the city, making a snowman with snow that will not be white for long, and observed by that other city dweller, the alley cat.

Glackens, for all his bravado, was known to love the atmosphere of sparkling mirrored restaurants and red-upholstered theaters. The fact that he admired the Impressionists can be seen in much of his work following his trip to France. *Hammerstein's Roof Garden* (page 124), for example, was a place of entertainment in New York City; however, the graceful, glittering way in which Glackens has painted the tightrope-walking scene makes the well-dressed audience look as if it has just stepped in from a Paris boulevard.

Other colorful young painters turned up regularly at Henri's Tuesday nights. Everett Shinn (1876–1953) loved the theater in every form—vaudeville, music halls, circuses, stage dramas, and the movies. For the Tuesday night gatherings at Henri's studio, Shinn began to write skits to be performed by members of the circle. Everyone screamed with laughter at his short comedies such as *Lucy Moore, or the Prune Hater's Daughter* or his takeoff of the popular

Hammerstein's Roof Garden, by
William J. Glackens, c. 1901.
*Oil on canvas. Collection of
Whitney Museum of American
Art*

drama *Trilby,* with Sloan playing the heroine in
a long frizzy wig, Henri playing the mad villain,
and Shinn himself appearing as a great American
painter living in Europe called "James McNails
Whiskers." This, obviously, was poking fun at
Whistler, which was typical of Henri's group.
Despite the fact that they all admired Whistler's
work, Henri and his friends made a point of never
taking famous figures too seriously.

Shinn's theatrical tastes are reflected in
many of his pictures. In 1901, journeying through
Europe, he attended performances of every kind.
In his painting of the *London Hippodrome,* an
English variety-show theater, he has captured a
trapeze artist in the dazzling glare of the stage
lights. The audience's various expressions can be
barely seen in the light that glows beneath the
gilded plaster and red-plush balcony in which

they are happily packed. Later in his career,
Shinn went to Hollywood and designed sets for
movies.

George Benjamin Luks (1867–1933) was
a rather mysterious young man who told Henri's
Tuesday night friends that he had once been a
boxer known to his faithful fans as "Lusty Luks"
and "Chicago Whitey, the Terror of the Windy
City." Even if he had enjoyed a career as a professional actor at one time, his newfound friends
refused to believe that he had ever been a barn-
storming fighter. He was given an opportunity
in 1895 to show off his courage, however, when he
joined Glackens in Cuba to record the thunderous
events of the Spanish-American War.

Luks was born in the heart of the Pennsylvania coal-mining district. His father, who was
a doctor, and his mother both liked to paint. It

London Hippodrome, by Everett Shinn, 1902   *Courtesy of the Art Institute of Chicago*

is not known whether George was first instructed by them. In fact, his life from the time he reached sixteen until past his twenty-sixth birthday remains something of a mystery to this day; but it seems to have been the raw, red-blooded life enjoyed by most of The Eight. In 1883 Luks left home with his brother in hopes of going on the stage as a vaudeville performer. He probably succeeded, and it is believed that for the next nine or ten years he traveled about in one way or another through England, France, and Germany. In 1894, he returned to Philadelphia, found a job as an illustrator for the *Philadelphia Press,* and joined Henri's circle of friends.

Comic strips made an overnight success in New York in 1896. Colored "funnies" were introduced to readers as eight pages that would make "the rainbow look like a lead pipe." The humor was extremely violent, and many parents protested. How "funny" some of these strips would appear today is doubtful. In one, a dog was made to solemnly say, "No man ever got wheat who planted weeds. Laziness is a mental disease." The first comic-strip hero was *The Yellow Kid.*

When its creator was hired away by a competing newspaper, Luks was invited to step in to fill his shoes. The next year, 1897, Glackens and Shinn arrived in New York to join Luks as illustrators at the paper; and in 1900 Henri himself settled in the city and became a teacher at the New York School of Art. It was Glackens who nagged Luks to start painting. Taking his advice, Luks set to work and began producing paintings of the farm and mining-town people with whom he had passed his childhood. Old women tending hens and geese came back to him from the past, along with sturdy laborers such as we see in Luks' portrait of a gruff coal miner puffing on a pipe, a torch strapped to his peaked cap, his canteen and lunch pail dangling from a blackened fist (page 126).

Luks worked swiftly with strong, bold brush strokes. He claimed that he could paint with a shoestring dipped in lard and tar if he had to. "Guts! Guts! Life! Life!" That is what he said his oil paintings were meant to express. In New York he looked for life in the poor neighborhoods of the city, in dancing children, and in the wrestling ring. In later years he became an art teacher, but

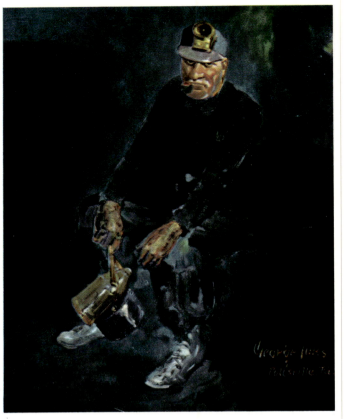

The Miner, by George Luks, 1925 *National Gallery of Art, Washington, D.C. Gift of Chester Dale*

his behavior was always more rowdy than that of his wildest students. He could never resist getting into a public brawl. Finally, poor Luks' body was found one morning in a doorway. Because of his reputation, his friends were afraid that he had died violently.

When they were reunited in New York, Henri's Tuesday night friends, Sloan, Glackens, Shinn and Luks, became the core of The Eight. They were joined by Ernest Lawson (1873–1939), Maurice Prendergast (1859–1924), and Arthur B. Davies (1862–1928), although the paintings of the last three had little in common with those of the original five. Lawson composed city views in thick layers of bright paint, and Prendergast painted sunny scenes with an Impressionist's delight. Davies created mysterious and calm "Romantic" landscapes.

One of Henri's pupils at the New York School of Art was George Bellows (1882–1925), who was destined to become one of the most popular painters in America for the first forty years of the twentieth century.

George Wesley Bellows was born in Columbus, Ohio, in 1882. By the time he reached the age of fifteen he stood six feet two inches tall and was a star of both his high school basketball and baseball teams. But his passion was drawing.

After high school Bellows entered Ohio State College, where the poetry of Walt Whitman and the plays of the Irish-English writer George Bernard Shaw made him aware of the problems of injustice and poverty. Bellows raised his voice with others in the demand for social change. In early twentieth-century America, the motto was "Every man for himself"; few had sympathy for the poor who could not rise from the terrible slums in which they were forced to live. At this time laborers had begun to unite and to strike for higher wages. Their employers often used cruel means to stop the new unions from organizing. Also, in the South, there was a sudden, terrible outbreak of racial violence. All these things led Bellows to become a lifelong fighter for human rights. In New York, he would soon discover that both Henri and Sloan felt as he did. Even so, the art of Bellows, Henri, and other "social realists" of the period served more as reports of real life in the city than as a criticism of unfair social conditions.

Once in New York, Bellows lost no time seeing everything he could. He rode the subways that had just been opened and the elevated trains that; powered by steam, rattled along two-story-high tracks. He gaped at the amazing Flatiron Building, the city's first skyscraper, and prowled through the streets of the lower East Side where immigrants shouting in foreign languages sold food, clothes, and other merchandise from clumsy pushcarts. He painted scenes of naked boys swimming in the East River, noisy prizefights, the back rooms of smoky saloons, dock workers and their huge horses, and bustling streets strung with colorful laundry on crisscrossing lines.

Bellows had earned the money to study in New York by drawing illustrations and cartoons for an Ohio newspaper and by playing semiprofessional baseball. The rapid sketches he had made for the paper helped him develop a painting style that we can see clearly in the picture *Both Members of This Club.* Prizefighting was then officially against the law in New York. To avoid the regulations, saloons would call themselves "private clubs" and sell tickets to "members." In Bellows' painting we can sense the sweaty violence of the fight, and hear the earsplitting cries of the specta-

Both Members of this Club, by George Bellows, 1909 *National Gallery of Art, Washington, D.C. Gift of Chester Dale*

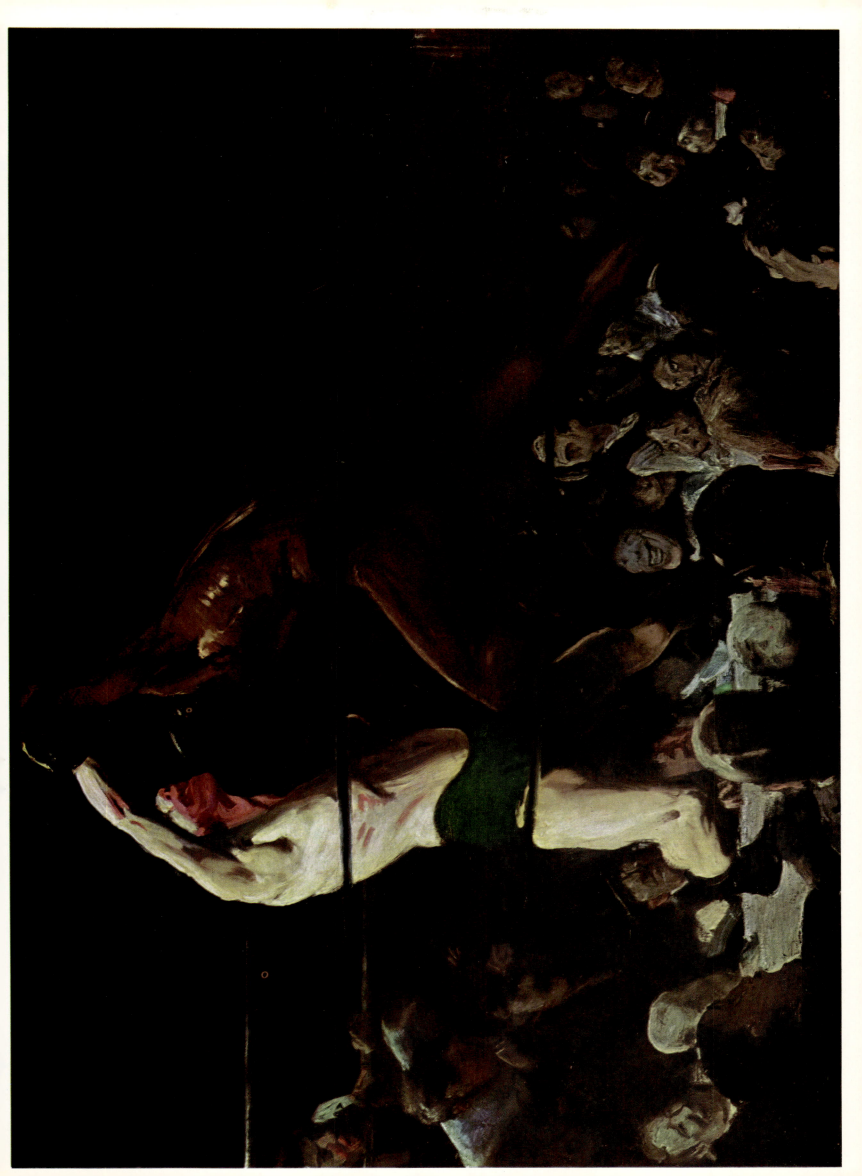

tors and the heavy thuds of leather gloves striking bruised jaws and bodies. In a quieter, sadder mood, Bellows recorded the chilly loneliness of the city on a wintry day in *The Lone Tenement*. Here, a tugboat puffs along merrily in the distance, making the solitary building and forlorn group of idle men trying to warm themselves seem even more alone and unhappy.

Bellows died tragically at the age of forty-three. Carrying his coffin were his old friends Henri, Sloan, Glackens, Prendergast, and Lawson, all members of The Eight. His death was seen as a national loss.

New Ideas from Abroad

It has been said that Bellows was "the most American of painters." Unlike his friends among The Eight, he had never gone abroad to study European art. He had never felt the need to copy anybody else's ideas, although he did express his admiration for the experiments of several artists working in Paris.

From the beginning of the twentieth century, Paris acted as a magnet for new generations of artists. They arrived not only from America, but also from Spain, Holland, Germany, Italy, Russia, and other countries. Although they came to work, study, and experiment, they could not help bringing with them the old ideas and traditions of their native lands. The combination of old and new styles and ideas created a wonderfully exciting atmosphere in which young artists might work. They visited each others' studios, prowled through museums and galleries, and spent many friendly hours in cafés discussing art.

It was Paris that had led the world when the Impressionists first broke with older styles of painting reality to achieve the reality of light and color. The Impressionists were followed by a group called the "Post-Impressionists," who strove to get meaning back into their pictures, to use this new light and color to express emotions and the inner nature of things. Now, in the early twentieth century, Paris was still at the forefront, and one startling development followed another.

Shortly before World War I, a small group of artists decided that it was time the American public saw the work of new artists, American and foreign alike. They set about organizing an exhibition. Their plans were greeted enthusiastically, and soon the group grew to include Davies, Glackens, Lawson, Luks, Henri, Bellows, Prendergast, Sloan, and the sculptor Jo Davison. The show was to take place in the huge, fortress-like Armory where New York's 69th Regiment held its drills.

Finally, more than thirteen hundred works of art were brought together, two-thirds of them by American artists. Glackens chose an American group which included several older painters, among them Whistler and Ryder. Ryder had been neglected to the point of being totally forgotten by the public, so it was with great joy that he was able to attend the Armory Show and see his paintings so well exhibited.

The Armory Show of 1913 caused an uproar. The press howled, the public was outraged. The paintings from Paris stole the show. The President of the United States, Teddy Roosevelt himself, said that the picture that most infuriated the public, Marcel Duchamp's *Nude Descending a Staircase*, looked like a Navajo blanket.

The Armory Show, in a somewhat smaller form, was sent to Chicago and Boston just as Europe was about to enter into a brutally destructive world war. The Americans joined the Allies in fighting the Germans in 1917, an experience that certainly made Americans more aware of Europe than they had been since the War of 1812. In 1918 an armistice was signed that halted the bloody battles.

Shortly afterward, in the 1920s, American painters, writers, poets, sculptors, and architects flocked to Europe in ever larger numbers. Paris was still considered the art capital of the world; it was where artists wanted to live and work. What, then, were these new, revolutionary movements in art which so outraged the American public, and so fascinated its artists?

The most startling new developments in Paris during the early years of the century were the revolutionary paintings of the "Fauves" and the "Cubists." *Fauves* (rhymes with "wove") is French for "wild beasts." This is what the critics

The Lone Tenement, by George Bellows, 1909
National Gallery of Art, Washington, D.C. Gift of Chester Dale

Zirchow VII, by Lyonel Feininger, 1918   *National Gallery of Art, Washington, D.C. Gift of Julia Feininger*

called a group of young painters who dared, with a loose free hand, to paint things any color they choose: a face could be green, a sky could be red, a field could be blue if the artist so decided. Their unofficial leader, Henri Matisse, explained that colors can act upon the feelings "like a sharp blow on a gong . . . the artist must be able to sound them when he needs to."

The inventors of "Cubism" were the Spaniard Pablo Picasso and the Frenchman George Braque. In Cubist painting, the artists tried to look at their subjects from many different angles. No longer were they content to look at a subject "head on," as a camera is obliged to do. Now they wanted to paint figures and objects from the top, bottom, sides, and back, all at the same time. This they tried to do by breaking up their subjects into many different surfaces or "planes." The final effect looked to many people like paintings of cubes and boxes tumbling in space.

The Cubists first invented "collage." *Collage* comes from the French word for "to paste." Collages are made by pasting different bits of paper, cloth, wood, sequins, labels—in fact any-thing that the artist's imagination suggests—to a canvas, board, or paper. The artist may also include areas of his own painting or drawing in his collage. The brilliant colors of the Fauves, the tumbling forms of the Cubists, and the development of collage all would have an extremely important influence on future modern artists.

The influence of Cubism can be seen clearly in *Zirchow VII,* a painting by New York-born Lyonel Feininger (1871–1956). Looking closely, we can see that Feininger has taken one of his favorite subjects, pointed church steeples and tall pitched roofs, as the painting's theme. Red roofs and pale buildings seem to shoot off into planes of deep blue sky and emerald green grass.

The paintings of the Fauves leader, Henri Matisse, and of the future Cubist Pablo Picasso, were first shown to Americans not at the Armory show, but at a small New York gallery owned by Alfred Stieglitz (1864–1946). By 1900, Stieglitz was considered the world's most outstanding amateur photographer. He was the founder and editor of four daring publications on photography and the arts. In 1902 he also founded a group called

Region of Brooklyn Bridge Fantasy, by John Marin, 1932 *Watercolor. 18¾ × 22¼ inches.*
Collection of Whitney Museum of American Art

"Photo-Secession." He and his followers believed that photography was not merely a modern gimmick but the only new art form to have been developed in five thousand years.

In 1905, Stieglitz opened his gallery at 291 Fifth Avenue. Officially called the "Little Galleries of the Photo Secession," it came to be known by its much more simple address number—"291." Between 1905 and 1917, Stieglitz presented more than seventy-five exhibitions of "avant-garde" artists (artists who are ahead of their times and who are leaders in new experiments). To the New York public, Stieglitz presented many young Americans who were indeed ahead of their times. Among them were John Marin (1870–1953), Arthur G. Dove (1880–1946), Charles Demuth (1883–1935), and Georgia O'Keeffe (born 1887).

Abstract Art

John Marin, born in Rutherford, New Jersey, is particularly well known for his watercolors of New York City and rocky seascapes of the Maine coast. After studying in Philadelphia and Paris, he was given an exhibition at the "291" in 1910. Stieglitz personally saw to it that Marin had money to live on while continuing his original, rather cubistic style of painting. Marin was excited by the soaring skyscrapers, the sweeping bridges, the flashing lights, and rushing rivers of New York, as can be seen in his *Region of Brooklyn Bridge Fantasy* (page 131).

Marin was among the first American artists to experiment with "abstract art." Cubism had taken a great step in the direction of purely abstract art, but generally, we can identify something of the original subject in a Cubist picture, such as the steep roofs in Feininger's painting. These objects have been "abstracted" to their basic lines and planes. In purely abstract art, all recognizable objects or figures have been banished from the painting, drawing, or sculpture. When we look at a piece of abstract art, we should no longer try to find shapes that are familiar to us. In abstract art, shapes, lines, and colors have a life and beauty of their own.

Perhaps the first true pioneer in American abstract painting was Arthur G. Dove. He, too, began his career as an illustrator in New York before visiting in Paris in 1908. In some of Dove's paintings, the forms that inspired him—sails, for example, or the moon—can be clearly seen, but in others which he called "extractions from nature," the subject has completely disappeared. He could even be inspired by sounds, such as in *Fog Horns*. Although the painting is an abstraction, the hovering shapes suggest to us the deep, echoing, warning groans of fog horns as they float mournfully out over the water. It was jokingly said of Dove:

> To show the pigeons would not do,
> And so he simply paints the coo.

Dove also liked to create "assemblages," cousins of collages, where various objects are arranged and tacked together within a framework. *Goin' Fishin'* is an assemblage of Huckleberry Finn objects—blue jeans, shirt, and bamboo fishing poles arranged in an abstract pattern that brings to mind a carefree summer afternoon spent on the shady bank of a stream.

It was a long time before paintings of "the coo" and assemblages of blue jeans and fishing poles would be appreciated by the public. Meanwhile, Dove, like Ryder before him, led a loner's life. He tried to support his family by chicken farming in Connecticut, but finally gave up. In ill health and dogged by money troubles, he spent his last years in an abandoned post office on Long Island, working to the very end. Dove wrote that, for him, art was always "a delightful adventure."

Charles Demuth was born in Lancaster, Pennsylvania. At eighteen, he left home to study art in Philadelphia and Paris, as Marin had done shortly before. He liked to work in watercolors, painting delicate, finely drawn pictures of grain elevators, flowers, landscapes, acrobats, and other vaudeville performers. About ten years before his death, he began a series of paintings he called "posters." One of these, *I Saw the Figure Five in Gold* (page 134), was inspired by a poem written by his friend William Carlos Williams. It was meant to be a "portrait" of Williams whose name appears in signs and twinkling lights at the top of

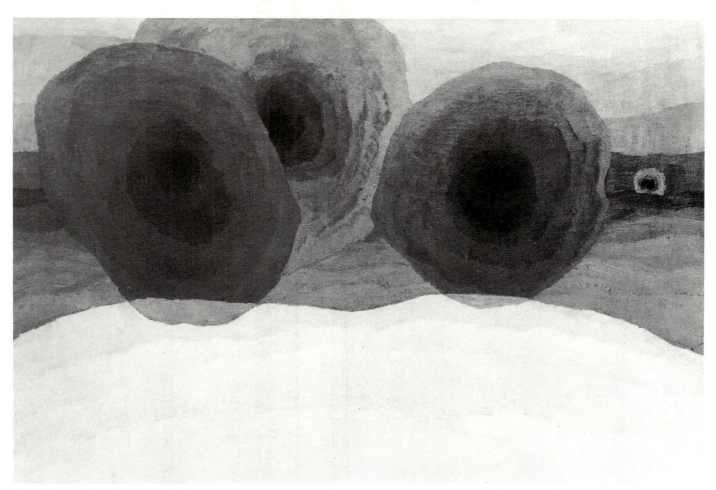

Fog Horns, by Arthur G. Dove, 1929   *Colorado Springs Fine Arts Center. Gift of Oliver B. James*

Goin' Fishin', by Arthur G. Dove, 1925   *The Phillips Collection, Washington, D.C.*

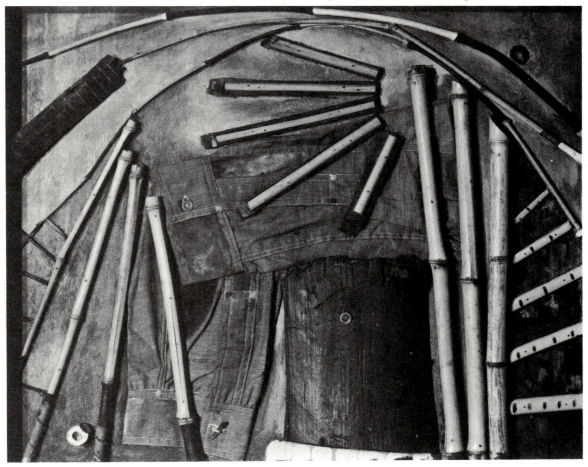

I Saw the Figure Five in Gold, by Charles Demuth, 1928   *The Metropolitan Museum of Art. The Alfred Stieglitz Collection, 1949*

the picture ("BILL" . . . "CARLO"). The poster recalls a shrieking fire engine tearing through the city streets on a dark, wet night:

> Among the rain
> and lights
> I saw the figure 5
> in gold
> on a red
> firetruck
> moving
> tense
> unheeded
> to gong clangs
> siren howls
> and wheels rumbling
> through the dark city.

One of the most outstanding of twentieth-century American artists to first exhibit at the "291" eventually married Alfred Stieglitz in 1924. Georgia O'Keeffe was her name, and she insisted on keeping it after their marriage. Never would she answer to the name "Mrs. Stieglitz." Independence was something that Georgia O'Keeffe has fought for throughout her long, active life.

Born in Sun Prairie, Wisconsin, O'Keeffe was twenty-six when, in 1913, she took a job in Texas as art supervisor in the Amarillo public schools. Surprisingly, she immediately loved the barren plains, the chilling winters, the haunting loneliness of the Texas Panhandle. "I lived on the plains of North Texas for four years," she later

134

explained. "It is the only place I have ever felt that I really belonged—that I really felt at home. . . . That was my country—terrible winds and a wonderful emptiness."

While in Texas, O'Keeffe made a series of charcoal drawings in an abstract style that was completely new to her. Until then she had worked as she had been taught, which meant that she dutifully copied nature as others did. Suddenly, she realized that "I had a lot of things in my head that others didn't have. . . . I made up my mind to put down what was in my head." O'Keeffe sent the results to a friend in New York for safekeeping, asking that she show them to no one. But when the friend saw the drawings, she thought that they were so excellent and original that she broke her promise and took them directly to Stieglitz. Stieglitz was equally impressed and hung several of them on the walls at "291," along with works of other artists.

When O'Keeffe heard what her friend had done, she was furious and demanded that the drawings be taken down immediately. Stieglitz tried to calm her and finally persuaded her to have her own exhibition at "291" the following year. After that, their happy association continued until Stieglitz's death in 1946.

For subject matter, O'Keeffe's paintings usually take giant flowers, skyscrapers, or vast New Mexico desert scenes rolling away into the distance behind bleached animal skulls or Spanish iron crosses such as the one in *Black Cross, New Mexico.*

The White Trumpet Flower (page 136) shows the center of a flower to be like a mysterious world of its own. "A flower," she has said, "touches almost everyone's heart. A red hill doesn't touch everyone's heart as it touches mine and I suppose there is no reason why it should. . . . All the earth colors of the painter's palette are out there in the many miles of bad lands . . . You have no associations with those hills—our wasteland—I think our most beautiful country." It is O'Keeffe's deep love and understanding of the Southwest that has brought to American art a collection of paintings that makes us also see the beauty of the country's barren deserts.

Black Cross, New Mexico, by Georgia O'Keeffe, 1929 *Courtesy of the Art Institute of Chicago*

The White Trumpet Flower, by Georgia O'Keeffe, 1932   *By permission,*
Georgia O'Keeffe. Fine Arts Gallery of San Diego. Gift of Inez Grant Parker
in memory of Earle W. Grant

Stella, Kuhn, and Hopper

Joseph Stella (1877–1946), Walt Kuhn (1880–1949), and Edward Hopper (1882–1967) were three young American artists whose work was shown at the famous Armory show. This 1913 exhibition introduced New Yorkers to a huge number of modern works.

All three men were very much painters of the American scene, which they saw in new and very different ways. Of the three, only Stella was fascinated by abstract art. For Kuhn and Hopper, like Bellows and Eakins before them, it was always human life and human emotions that were important.

Walt Kuhn was born in Brooklyn, and dropped out of school to open a bicycle shop. In many ways, his life was like those of The Eight, who later became his friends. He entered bicycle races at country fairs, and in his spare time drew cartoons for a San Francisco newspaper. Finally, in 1901, he went to study in Paris and Germany.

Kuhn's pictures, particularly those painted after the Armory Show, frequently used powerful figures of clowns and acrobats as subjects. *The Blue Clown* (page 138) is typical of his style. Kuhn's clowns have a strong sense of dignity, but beneath their whitened faces we see expressions of sadness, anger, or dismay, that "realism" of the human soul we saw in the tired faces of Eakins portraits. Kuhn, in the 1920s, designed and directed musical shows six months of the year. The other six months he would spend earnestly painting. Later he even designed club cars for railroads. He always tended to overwork, and as a tragic result, he suffered a nervous collapse and died in a mental hospital.

Edward Hopper (1882–1967) was one of Robert Henri's most talented pupils. He studied for several years in Paris before exhibiting in the Armory Show, where he sold his first picture. Hopper, too, dwelled on human emotions, and above all on the subject of loneliness, particularly the loneliness of life in the city. He was the first painter to capture the unhappiness of Americans on the move from one place to another without an end in view. He closely observed the sadness of cheap hotel rooms, empty movie theaters, rows of cheerless houses, and tired people sitting in all-night cafés. *Nighthawks,* for example, shows us just such a forlorn scene. Hopper would memorize details of what he saw on his travels around the country and would later put them together in unforgettable pictures conjured up from both his memory and his imagination.

For Joseph Stella, on the other hand, human emotions and the human figure mattered little. Stella was born in Italy, near the city of Naples, but moved to New York at the age of nineteen. There he became a magazine illustrator. While working for a publication called *The Survey,* he was asked to draw pictures of the steel and coal industries in Pittsburgh. This experience over-whelmed him. He believed that American industrial progress must be the subject for his art. Return trips to Europe had made him familiar with the newest experiments in painting, and he saw the "abstract" beauty in the towering structures of industry. As a result he developed a bold personal style to express the energy of the industrial age with its miracles of building and engineering. *The Brooklyn Bridge: Variation on an Old Theme* (page 138) glows with different shafts and twinkles of artificial light. Glaring lights strike the swooping metal arcs of the great bridge; softer lights glow from countless windows in the towering shadows of the New York skyline. Like Kuhn's clowns and Hopper's lonely streets, Stella's iron shapes were portraits of the twentieth century.

A Homegrown American Art

There were many who felt that the influence of European art and European ideas had gone too far in America.

Nighthawks, by Edward Hopper, 1942   *Courtesy of the Art Institute of Chicago*

The Brooklyn Bridge: Variation on an Old Theme, by Joseph Stella, 1939 *Oil on canvas. 70 × 42 inches. Collection of Whitney Museum of American Art*

The need for a truly American art was pointed out repeatedly by the historian and critic Thomas Craven. Craven was encouraged by those painters "who have looked beyond their studio walls into the fascinating American environment, whose pictures point out the road which our artists must travel in order to deliver themselves from European masquerade and create something of their own." He singled out Bellows and Sloan for special praise. Craven suggested that other Americans follow their example and look to their own country instead of Europe for artistic inspiration.

Three painters who agreed wholeheartedly with Craven were Thomas Hart Benton (1889–1975), Grant Wood (1892–1941), and John Steuart Curry (1897–1946). Today they are usually known as "Regionalists" or "American Scene" painters because of the homegrown subject matter of their pictures.

Born in the small midwestern town of Neosho, Missouri, Thomas Hart Benton was the son of a United States congressman and the grand-

The Blue Clown, by Walt Kuhn, 1931 *Oil on canvas. 104 × 70 inches. Collection of Whitney Museum of American Art*

nephew of a well-known senator. With this background, it is not surprising that Benton would develop a deep interest in American history.

Typical midwestern farm scenes were among Benton's favorite subjects. Sunburned farmers and sturdy work horses, furrowed fields and sparkling streams, gnarled trees and whispering wheat fields, golden in the bright midwestern sunshine, reappear like glowing reminders of America's "good old days." *Cradling Wheat* (page 140) shows farmers threshing wheat by hand. A boy is helping them bind or "cradle" the grain in the late summer light of harvest time.

Grant Wood was born on an Iowa farm. His most famous painting, *American Gothic* (page 140), sums up in the minds of millions of Americans the lives and character of hardworking, down-to-earth Iowa farm people. Wood made four trips to Europe between World War I and 1930. There, he was deeply impressed by the finely detailed pictures that the old Flemish masters had painted nearly five hundred years before. As a young man, Wood had earned his living as a maker of miniature model houses. In *American Gothic,* we can see three of the major interests and influences of

his life—the plain faces and neat homes of Iowa farmers, the Flemish masters' love of tiny details (seen here, for example, in the wife's cameo brooch and rickrack-trimmed apron, the potted plants, the husband's gold collar button, the lace curtain hanging in the Gothic Revival window), and the dollhouse quality of the buildings.

John Steuart Curry's parents were devoutly religious Kansas farm people. After studying art in the Midwest, he moved to New York and became a successful magazine illustrator. In 1926 he went to Paris for a year. On his return to New York he painted *Baptism in Kansas,* one of the first in a dramatic series depicting the life he had known back home on the farm. Here we see a young woman about to be immersed in a baptismal font made of wooden staves, much like an oversize bucket or horse trough. Hymns are sung as a small group of adults and children dressed in white await their turn to be baptized by a rugged old preacher standing knee deep in the water. Behind the heads of the congregation can be glimpsed the broken-down cars that have brought them to this religious ceremony in a Kansas farmyard.

Baptism in Kansas, by John Steuart Curry, 1928   *Oil on canvas. 40 × 50 inches.*
Collection of Whitney Museum of American Art

Cradling Wheat, by Thomas Hart Benton, 1938   *The St. Louis Art Museum*

American Gothic, by Grant Wood, 1930   *Courtesy of the Art Institute of Chicago*

Andrew Wyeth (b. 1917), the Pennsylvania-born artist, might also be called a "regionalist painter." The son of a famous illustrator, Wyeth seems to have learned something of art from his father, although in many ways he was self-taught. Wyeth's work, in soft shades of tempera with thousands of fine brush strokes, creates extremely realistic portraits and landscapes. Many of his pictures seem touched with quiet sadness. The lined faces of old neighbors, the chipped dignity of Pennsylvania farm houses, the daydreaming expressions of young people on the brink of growing up are each given Wyeth's careful attention in cool, almost photographically detailed paintings. His most famous work is a strangely touching picture of a girl crippled by polio crawling through the brown stubble of a Pennsylvania field in search of berries. Called *Christina's World,* this picture makes us feel, with Christina, that she is trapped in the lonely emptiness of a world which for her stops at the boundary lines of a grim, treeless farm.

Christina's World, by Andrew Wyeth, 1948   *Tempera on gesso panel. 32¼ × 47¾. Collection, The Museum of Modern Art, New York*

Architecture

Meanwhile, scientific and technical advances were changing, in unheard-of ways, the simple life the Regionalists painted. Speed records were broken again and again. Assembly lines produced more goods than ever before. Automobiles, trains, ships, and airplanes had to be redesigned for faster travel. This dynamic new age would see the rise of "industrial designers" such as Norman Bel Geddes (1893–1958). Born in Michigan, Bel Geddes began his artistic career as a stage and film designer. By 1927, he had set up his own studio for industrial design. It was he who introduced the word "streamline" to the language. By "streamlining" he was referring to his sleek new shapes for trains and ships, automobiles and airplanes. These were specially designed to reduce friction and thereby increase speed. Bel Geddes soon was "streamlining" everything from refrigerators and stoves to bottles and a whole "House for Tomorrow."

Architecture had also undergone a revolu-

tion that was completely American. As we have seen, during the nineteenth century, architects had repeated and adapted designs of the past: the Classical Revival, the Gothic Revival. The "modern" streamlined world of the twentieth century needed something totally new. This need was filled by a great American innovator, Frank Lloyd Wright (1869–1959).

Wright was born in Wisconsin, the son of a Baptist minister, and left his family at the age of sixteen. He took a job with a local builder, studied engineering, and at eighteen went to work for a Chicago architect. His talent was immediately recognized, and soon he was working on his own, designing buildings in a spectacularly new style. If we compare the Robie House, designed by Wright in 1909, with the kind of Gothic Revival building still being constructed at the time, we can see at a glance how extraordinarily new Wright's design is. What inspired this total change, this invention of a "modern" architecture by Wright?

Fifty years earlier, Commodore Perry's expedition had opened Japan to American visitors.

Robie House, Chicago, Illinois, designed by Frank Lloyd Wright, 1908–09 *Photograph, Courtesy of The Museum of Modern Art, New York*

The Japanese later were persuaded to exhibit examples of their art and architecture at an international fair held in the United States. The long, low horizontal lines, uncluttered surfaces, and overhanging eaves of the Japanese building style must have impressed Wright deeply. He also loved the simple cubelike forms of children's playing blocks recently invented by the educator Froebel, forms which resembled the new "cubistic" paintings. The "cantilevered" roofs and terraces, projecting far from the central core of Wright's buildings, are completely his own. Wright had taken the feeling of the new art, which broke down forms into "abstract" planes, and brought it to architecture even before abstract art came into being.

Of course, the great architectural form of the twentieth century is the skyscraper. With tremendous growth and industrialization, many cities, especially New York, by now the country's largest, were forced to grow upward. New steel superstructures and passenger elevators now enabled architects to build to any height. At first they did not know how to handle these soaring new giants, and so they simply added old architectural decorations to the new buildings, usually at the top. So Gothic cathedrals, Italian palaces, and Greek temples hovered in midair. By the 1930s, it was clear that newer, more streamlined forms, were needed. The Empire State Building, constructed in 1931 and for many decades the world's

142

tallest building, is an example. By the 1950s, however, new materials enabled architects to open the walls of their buildings with great glass surfaces. The slablike form and clean lines of Lever House, built in 1952, foretold the architecture to come.

Lever House, New York, designed by Skidmore, Owings and Merrill, 1952 *Photo courtesy of Skidmore, Owings and Merrill, N.Y.C.*

The Passion of Sacco and Vanzetti, by Ben Shahn, 1931–32   *From the Sacco and Vanzetti Series of 23 paintings. Tempera. 84½ × 48 inches. Collection of Whitney Museum of American Art. Gift of Edith and Milton Lowenthal in memory of Juliana Force*

The Great Depression

Despite the new power of American industry and the streamlined world, life was grim for countless Americans during the 1930s. Financial disasters in 1929 ended with millions of people unemployed. Throughout the country there were endless lines of men and women waiting for work, or for bread. This was the Great Depression. It affected artists just as much as businessmen and factory workers, or perhaps more, as art has always been considered a luxury. In 1933, President Franklin Roosevelt came to the artists' aid and established the Public Works of Art Project, which was followed by the Works Progress Administration (WPA). These federal agencies supported thousands of artists, who were each given a small weekly salary. Many were put to work decorating the walls of public buildings. In a way this was an extraordinary stroke of luck for painters who otherwise could not have afforded to work experimentally, even in better times.

Among the many who were helped by the WPA was a group of young artists who were distressed by social conditions in the United States. They have come to be known as "social protest" painters, because their art did more than merely show poverty, as had the paintings of The Eight. It showed, too, injustice at work and the artists' strong protest against suffering that was harsher than ever during the depression. One of these painters was Ben Shahn (1898–1969).

Ben Shahn's family had a history of social protest. Born in Lithuania, Shahn's father had been sent to Siberia for plotting against the Russian Czar. He escaped and eventually managed to bring his family to New York. Shahn was later apprenticed to a printer in Brooklyn, and in 1925 made his first return trip to Europe. Back once more in New York, he was shocked by the executions of Sacco and Vanzetti, two Italian immigrants whose revolutionary political beliefs led to their execution for a murder they almost certainly had not committed. The Sacco-Vanzetti case disturbed Shahn deeply, and he decided to record the tragic story in pictures. "Here I was living through another crucifixion," said Shahn. "Here was something to paint!" Seven months

144

later, he had completed twenty-three pictures of their story, one of which is *The Passion of Sacco and Vanzetti* (page 143). Here the two men are shown in their coffins before a courthouse, the victims of injustice. Shahn also painted social protest pictures showing the painful lives of coal miners, labor leaders, and blacks.

Jacob Lawrence (b. 1917) was brought from Philadelphia to Harlem in 1929, in his early teens. He had moved from the South to the North in the 1920s and '30s, a member of one of the many families searching for work and a better life. The Harlem to which he came was bursting with vitality, and with art. During the 1920s Harlem had become famous for its dance halls, theaters, cafés, and for its writers, musicians, and artists. With many painters and sculptors, it had an art world of its own.

Young Lawrence took odd jobs after school

No. 6 of John Brown Series, by Jacob Lawrence, 1941
Courtesy of The Detroit Institute of Arts

hours—he delivered newspapers, and worked in a laundry, a bakery, and a print shop. But from the beginning it was art that interested him most of all. Soon after his arrival, the depression set in. It was felt even more in Harlem than elsewhere. Men were without work; and the lively, exciting days of the 1920s were a thing of the past. Fortunately, at the WPA's Harlem Art Workshop, the best of the Harlem artists, such as Augusta Savage and Charles Alston, were able to teach talented students like young Lawrence, who had his first exhibition at the 135th Street YMCA when he was just twenty-one.

Lawrence set out to present in his painting the heritage of his people, and the black struggle for liberty. He painted events in black history, the stories of Toussaint L'Ouverture, the liberator of Haiti, Frederick Douglass, Harriet Tubman, John Brown, and of the migration of blacks from the South to the North, which he felt to be a great national movement. Look at painting *No. 6* from the John Brown series. Here is the story of John Brown's attack on the federal arsenal at Harper's Ferry. The scene is broken up into a flat abstract pattern, and the jagged shapes tell the agony of the struggle. But it is not only the struggle of blacks. It is the human struggle of man himself "always to better his conditions and to move forward" that is for Lawrence the most important theme in art.

Jack Levine (b. 1915) paints in an impressionistic style that is very personal. In his pictures he tries, as he has put it, to "do something for the world." *Gangster Funeral* is typical of his work. Here we see a gangster laid out in a funeral parlor. Paying their respects are policemen and politicians, and we see that, in their self satisfied way, they are on the best of terms with the underworld.

Gangster Funeral, by Jack Levine, 1952–53   *Oil on canvas. 63 × 72 inches. Collection of Whitney Museum of American Art*

One (Number 31, 1950), by Jackson Pollock, 1950   *Oil and enamel on canvas.*
8'10" × 17'5⅝". Collection, The Museum of Modern Art, New York.
Gift of Sidney Janis

Abstract Expressionism

The year 1939 saw the beginning of a great cataclysm that almost destroyed Europe and left the United States at the forefront of world art.

Trouble had begun in the early 1930s, when Adolf Hitler and his Nazi followers made life increasingly difficult for German experimental artists. Hitler declared that all forms of expressionism and abstract painting were "diseased," the work of sick minds and madmen. With the coming of war, many artists fled to America from countries seized and crushed by Hitler. In fact, much of the best European art was transplanted in the United States and served as a great inspiration to young American artists about to develop new movements of their own.

With "Abstract Expressionism," probably America's most important modern movement, Americans took the lead in world art. Arshile Gorky, who came to America from Armenia at the age of sixteen, was perhaps a pioneer in this direction (although he was not aware of it at the time).

His painting entitled simply *Painting* suggests dream shapes in a dream space. It was the Abstract Expressionist's intention to bring the emotions of Expressionism to abstract art.

The group of painters known as "Abstract Expressionists" seem at times to have little in common. But as we have already seen, group names such as the "Ash Can School" are sometimes invented simply as a convenient way of identifying a loosely connected circle of artists, whether their works are similar or not.

Jackson Pollock (1912–1956), who was born in Cody, Wyoming, attracted more attention in the years immediately following his accidental death than any American artist since George Bellows. The reason for this partly lay in the strong reactions of Americans to his famous "dribble" paintings, created by dripping and splashing swirls, blobs, and splatters of paint on increasingly larger canvases. These bore little resemblance to the pictures he had painted many years earlier, as a student with the Regionalist artist Thomas Hart Benton. In *One*, we find a typical example of Pollock's style of "action painting." He said that

Painting, by Arshile Gorky, 1936–37   *Oil on canvas. 38 × 48 inches. Collection of Whitney Museum of American Art*

The Frozen Sounds, Number 1, by Adolph Gottlieb, 1951   *Oil on canvas. 36 × 48 inches. Collection of Whitney Museum of American Art. Gift of Mr. and Mrs. Samuel M. Kootz*

a painting has a life of its own—"I try to let it come through." Pollock also once said that the only American artist who ever interested him was Ryder, the great "Romantic" painter. This statement lets us see Pollock's work in an interesting light. Have the raging moonlit clouds and fantastic deep heavens of Ryder's paintings in some way inspired the dramatic and magical swirls of Jackson Pollock's Abstract Expressionist art?

The term "action painting" suggests strenuous physical activity; it brings to mind the image of an artist attacking a canvas with all his energy in order to express his strongest feelings. This, indeed, is exactly what "action painting" is supposed to mean. Pollock, Willem de Kooning, and Franz Kline were "action painters" in the most passionate sense of the term. Each had been influenced by the idea of "automatic writing," the writing which comes automatically and unconsciously to the hand. They applied paint to canvas with the same directness as the "automatic writers" put words down on paper as they came into their heads. As a result, their emotions and energy have electrified each of their canvases with, as Pollock put it, "a life of its own."

Willem de Kooning's (b. 1904) Abstract Expressionist "action paintings" sometimes are based on easily identifiable subjects; *Woman and*

Woman and Bicycle, by Willem de Kooning, 1952–53
Oil on canvas. 76½ × 49 inches. Collection of Whitney Museum of American Art

Mahoning, by Franz Kline, 1956   *Oil on canvas. 80 × 100 inches. Collection of Whitney Museum of American Art. Gift of the Friends of the Whitney Museum of American Art*

Bicycle is an example of this style. Slashing smears of paint give de Kooning's picture an atmosphere of nervous violence and hidden danger. Here again, we have the feeling of strong emotions being expressed.

Franz Kline (1910–1962) spent his childhood, like Luks, in the heart of the Pennsylvania coal country. His most admired paintings are overpowering Abstract Expressionist studies in black and white. *Mahoning* is typical of Kline's strong style. "Does the emotion come across?" was the question he felt most important when judging a work of art. In *Mahoning*, we can say that it does.

Dreamlike landscapes, in beautiful colors, sprang from the imagination of Adolph Gottlieb (1903–1974). Gottlieb's long career began when he was a student of Robert Henri and John Sloan, proceeded through the 1930s with the help of the WPA, and blossomed into splendid new flower after World War II. *The Frozen Sounds Number 1* (page 147) presents a haunting universe in the free and imaginative style of the Abstract Expressionists. Other Abstract Expressionists noted for brilliant combinations of color that create either joyful, calm, or sorrowful moods are Mark Rothko (1903–1970), whose canvases of melting color are considered among the finest of Abstract Expressionist work, and Milton Resnick (b. 1917), whose enchanting *Genie* is seen on page 151.

Sculpture

Contemporary American sculptors have also broken new ground. American sculpture in the early years of the twentieth century tended to follow safe, traditional paths. An exception was Paris-born Gaston Lachaise (1882–1935) who wrote, "At twenty I met a young American person who immediately became the primary inspiration which awakened my vision and the leading influence that had directed my forces. Throughout my career, as an artist, I refer to this person by the word 'woman.'" This person was Isabel Nagel, a girl from Boston, and Lachaise soon followed her to the United States and married her. It was only then that he developed his own particular sculptural style, creating female figures of monumental bulk and solidity that appear, all the

Woman Walking, by Gaston Lachaise, 1922
Bronze. 18½" high, at base 6½ × 5⅜". Collection, The Museum of Modern Art, New York. Gift of Abby Aldrich Rockefeller

same, light and nimble. Lachaise was one of a number of American sculptors in the first half of the century who concentrated on sculpting the human figure, which they transformed into gracefully heroic shapes.

But soon American sculptors became fascinated with the idea of creating abstract shapes in sculptural form. Among the first were Alexander Calder (b. 1898), David Smith (1906–1965), and Isamu Noguchi (b. 1904). Calder, the son and grandson of sculptors, was born in Lawnton, Pennsylvania, and showed a remarkable talent for line drawing when he was still very young. In 1926 he moved into a small studio in Paris and began to create a wondrous circus and menagerie out of bent wire, scraps of cloth, bits of wood and metal, buttons, sequins, snippets of yarn, and other seemingly useless materials that fell into his inventive hands. Word went round that this remarkable young American was truly an artistic wizard. Soon many famous figures began dropping by Calder's studio to be bewitched by his tumblers and carnival dancers, trapeze artists and performing animals (page 152).

Crags and Critters, by Alexander Calder, 1974 *Courtesy Perls Galleries, New York*

Sculptures by Isamu Noguchi, photographed at the Whitney Museum of American Art. Left to right: Sesshu, 1959. Avatar, 1947. Endless Coupling, 1957. *Anodized aluminum, Georgia marble, cast iron. By permission of the artist. Photograph by Michio Noguchi, courtesy Pace Gallery*

Calder's early training as an engineer, he later said, made things simpler for him when he first set about inventing "mobiles." Mobiles are what his friend, Marcel Duchamp, called Calder's gently floating constructions suspended by fine wire often from a ceiling. In contrast to Calder's moving mobiles, his "stabiles" remain rooted to the ground. When asked what the basic difference is between his mobiles and stabiles, Calder explained, "You have to walk around a stabile or through it—a mobile dances in front of you." In *Crags and Critters* the sculptor has combined dangling mobiles with stabile craggy "mountains" and cavorting critters. Here even Calder's stabiles seem to dance.

The dramatic sculpture of Isamu Noguchi (b. 1904) may suggest either ancient mysteries (like the strange totemic spirits we have seen earlier), the changing moods of nature, or the awesome dignity of monumental art of the Far East. Noguchi's works may either bristle, stalk, writhe, bulge, shimmer, flash, or stand as serene as a silent high priest. Born in Los Angeles, Noguchi spent his childhood in his father's homeland, Japan. Long periods of study and work in the Orient, Europe, and America have encouraged him to experiment with many materials and techniques, old and new, as seen in the three contrasting abstract sculptures which were included in the Whitney Museum's 1968 review of Noguchi's many-sided career.

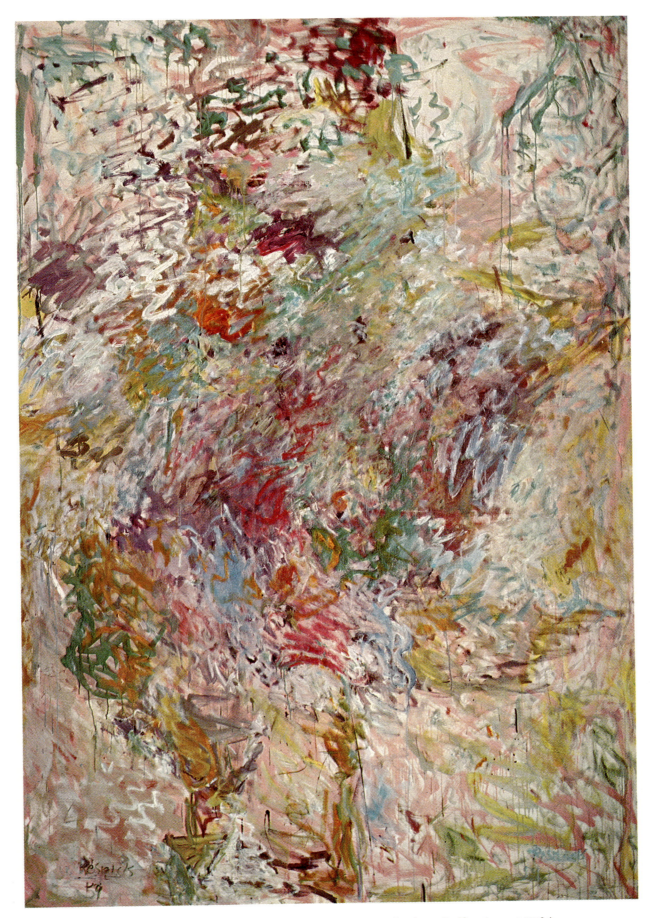

Genie, by Milton Resnick, 1959 *Oil on canvas. 104 × 70 inches. Collection of Whitney*
Museum of American Art

The Brass Family, by Alexander Calder, 1929   *Brass wire. 64 × 41 × 8½ inches. Collection of Whitney Museum of American Art. Gift of the artist*

Critics generally agree that the sculpture of David Smith (1906–1965) is one of the most original achievements in the history of American art. It is true that Calder had large sheets of steel cut into abstract shapes to form his mammoth stabiles. Smith went even further. He ran what amounted to a professional factory for the construction and welding together of his experimental sculpture precisely as if they were machines.

Smith, who was born in Decatur, Indiana, studied painting with John Sloan in New York. Sloan, like Henri, Luks, and Bellows, believed in "red-blooded" American art. In Smith, he found an ideal pupil. Smith had also been introduced to Cubism. He soon started to apply such thick, heavy layers of paint to his canvases that gradually they began to look more like sculpture than paintings. He attached bits of wood and other "found objects" to his pictures. It was clear by now that Smith was moving farther and farther

152

away from painting and into the field of sculpture. Next he produced painted wooden constructions that could stand upright by themselves.

Smith had once worked as a riveter in an automobile assembly line. It was therefore easy for

Lectern Sentinel, by David Smith, 1961   *Stainless steel. 101¾ × 33 × 20½ inches. Collection of Whitney Museum of American Art*

him to take his next experimental step into metal constructions. At first these new works were quite small. In 1940 he moved to a country village in New York State, near Lake George. There, in the middle of a serene landscape, he built his machine shop, which Smith nicknamed the "Terminal Iron Works." At the "Iron Works," his sculpture became increasingly monumental and abstract. At first, nature provided Smith with basic subjects to develop into large abstract sculpture. In his later years, Smith declared that "the artist is now his own nature, the work is the total art." Working in stainless steel, he created spectacular abstract sculptures such as *Lectern Sentinel*, which, along with his earlier works, have influenced sculptors around the world.

Louise Nevelson (b. 1900) was born in Russia but came to the United States as a small child, when her family settled on the Maine coast.

By twenty she was in New York, and studying many arts—drawing, painting, singing, and dramatics. Gradually, after travel and study in Europe and South America, she developed her own special style of abstract sculpture. She assembled bits of "found materials"—anything from a length of wall molding to shattered pieces of furniture, old tools, or even toilet seats. These "found materials" she often enclosed in square, boxlike shapes, which then would be cemented together and sprayed with one solid color of paint (black, white, or, during one period, gold). The results of Nevelson's assemblages have been called ageless and permanent "sculptural landscapes." In *Young Shadows*, shadows in fact play an important part in the sculpture. The shadows are cast by objects we may recognize from life, but they have been transformed into part of a powerful and mysterious sculptural whole.

Young Shadows, by Louise Nevelson, 1959–60 *Painted wood, 115 × 126 × 7¾ inches. Collection of Whitney Museum of American Art. Gift of the Friends of the Whitney Museum of American Art*

Green Coca Cola Bottles, by Andy Warhol, 1962   Oil on canvas. 82¼ × 57 inches. Collection of Whitney Museum of American Art. Gift of the Friends of the Whitney Museum of American Art

Still Life Number 36, by Tom Wesselmann, 1964   *Oil and collage on canvas. 120 × 192¼ inches.*
Collection of Whitney Museum of American Art. Gift of the artist

Pop Art

Time and again, realism has played an important part in the history of American art. What we call "Pop Art" began when a group of sculptors and painters who were not interested in abstract art began to play with realism in strange, unimagined new ways. Perhaps the first and surely the most famous Pop Artist was Andy Warhol (b. 1930). Warhol, who started his career as a commercial artist, became famous for depicting Campbell's Soup cans, coffee tins, movie stars, and Coca-Cola bottles. He has said that he likes to be bored, which may explain his repeated use of a single image in some of his pictures. Similarly, some of the early "underground" movies that he has filmed feature a man sleeping endlessly or the Empire State Building as seen from the same position for almost eight hours. Tom Wesselmann (b. 1931) is best known for his brightly colored nudes. In his giant oil and collage, however, called *Still Life Number 36,* he creates a billboard world of space-age still lifes—an enormous hero sandwich, a towering glass of milk, and a huge package of "modern cigarettes."

The sculptor George Segal (b. 1924) likes to create eerie scenes by combining real objects with plaster casts of live people. To produce these casts, Segal wraps live people in cloths soaked in wet plaster. This must be done in separate sections. When the plaster dries, Segal assembles the parts of his ghostly figures and places them in settings composed of real objects. *Girl in Doorway* is a typical example of Segal's unusual art (page 156).

Claes Oldenburg, born in Sweden in 1929 but brought up in Chicago, aims to create art which "takes its forms from life itself . . . and is sweet and stupid as life itself." Therefore we should not be surprised to find sprawling on a museum floor an enormous deflated telephone, a mammoth collapsing typewriter, or a seven-foot-wide snack such as his *Giant Hamburger*. These are in no way meant to be exact replicas of the original subjects; instead we see them as astonishing objects escaped from a dream, possibly a nightmare. Oldenburg's "soft sculptures," which appear to fall in upon themselves, are made from vinyl plastic and similar floppy substances. The sculptor's more solid looking constructions are composed of a variety of materials. *Giant Hamburger*, for example, is painted sailcloth stuffed with foam. And what could be more "sweet and stupid" than the real store which Oldenburg rented in which to display his extraordinary sculptured wares—

Girl in Doorway, by George Segal, 1965
Construction, plaster, wood, glass and aluminum paint. 113 × 63½ × 18 inches.
Collection of Whitney Museum of American Art

sausages, soda pop, cakes and breads, dresses, shirts and shoes, all made out of chicken wire, plaster and muslin daubed with shiny house paint.

Pop Art was the most successful artistic movement in America in the 1960s. Pop artists show the viewer mass-produced objects that he saw about him everyday, often images from commercial advertising that appear everywhere—on shop counters, television screens, billboards. Pop artists say to the public, "This is reality. You take this for granted. But have you ever really seen it? Have you ever really looked at it?" In a way, this is what every American realist was saying: Homer, who showed us the reality of the country and the sea; Eakins, who showed us the truth of the human spirit; The Eight, who showed us the reality of city life. Pop artists show us the reality of the commercial world in which we live.

"Pop Art" is only one of many movements in recent American art. The "Op" artists create optical illusions which trick the eye into seeing movement that does not actually take place. "Minimal" painters reduce their art to the simplest forms possible—flat shapes, flat colors, and pure

Giant Hamburger, by Claes Oldenburg, 1962 *Painted sailcloth stuffed with foam. 52″ × 84″ approximately.* *Art Gallery of Ontario. Purchase, 1967*

Circle Path, by Alexander Liberman, 1952 *Collection of the artist*

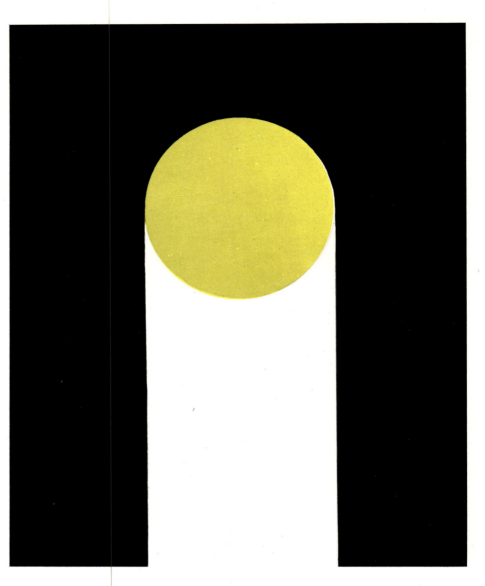

Atlantic, by Ellsworth Kelly, 1956   *Oil on canvas. 80 × 114 inches. Collection of Whitney Museum of American Art*

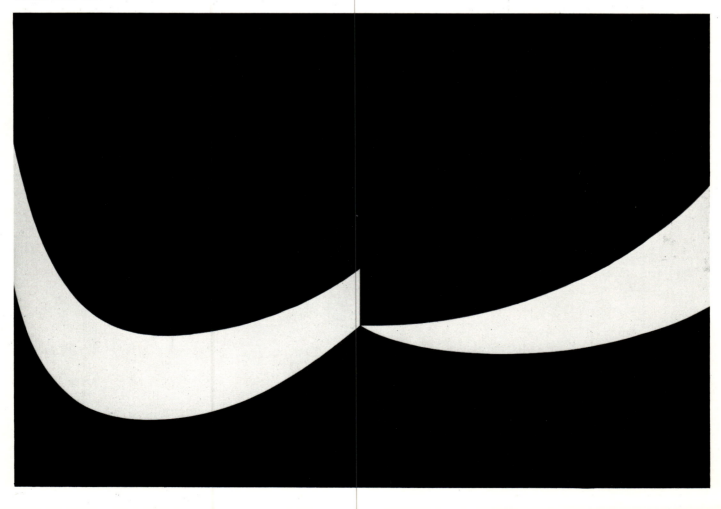

lines. The extremely simplified, "hard edged" shapes in *Circle Path* by Alexander Liberman (b. 1912) are typical of "minimal" art. Since 1950, Liberman has experimented with perfect compass-drawn circles, placing them against what may appear to be either a flat background or endless space. In some ways, *Circle Path* could also be seen as an early example of Op Art. Do we see a yellow disc soaring upward, leaving behind a white tail like a comet's, or do we simply see a plain, tube-like object? If so, do we see the object from within or without? Does the object turn itself inside out before our eyes?

Equally simplified, hard edged shapes are also found in Ellsworth Kelly's (b. 1923) *Atlantic.* Kelly was probably the first American artist to experiment with unusually shaped canvases, and to create inventive works of art by arranging series of panels together, each one painted a different solid color.

Artists of the "New Realism," still another recent movement, create paintings so realistic that they might be mistaken for photographs. *'61 Pontiac* by Robert Bechtle (b. 1932) may seem very different from *The Copley Family* (page 62), but it shows us that the American love of realism in art is still strong. And yet this is an age of constant experimentation, of questioning, of trying new forms. Every side of American life is being examined, studied, changed. And so American artists, too, are experimenting, changing. There have been many movements in American art, and certainly there will be more.

The American artist is always searching.

'61 Pontiac, by Robert Bechtle, 1968–69   Oil on canvas. 60 × 84 inches. Collection of Whitney Museum of American Art. Richard and Dorothy Rodgers Fund